A Colour Atlas of

AIDS

Acquired Immunodeficiency Syndrome

Charles F. Farthing, MB, ChB, MRCP
Research Registrar in AIDS,
St. Stephen's Hospital, London

Simon E. Brown, FIMBI, ABIPP, ARPS
Chief Photographer,
Charing Cross & Westminster Medical School, London

Richard C.D. Staughton, MA (Cantab), FRCP
Consultant Physician to the Skin Departments
Westminster and St. Stephen's Hospitals, London

Jeffrey J. Cream, BSc (Hons), MD, FRCP
Consultant Dermatologist,
Charing Cross Hospital, London

Mark Mühlemann, BSc (Hons), MB, BS, MRCP
Senior Registrar,
Department of Dermatology,
Charing Cross Hospital, London

Wolfe Medical Publications Ltd
Year Book Medical Publishers, Inc

Copyright © C. F. Farthing, S. E. Brown, R. C. D. Staughton, J. J. Cream,
M. Mühlemann, 1986
Published by Wolfe Medical Publications Ltd, 1986
Printed by W. S. Cowell Ltd, 8 Butter Market, Ipswich, England
Reprinted 1987
ISBN 07234 0954 4

For a full list of other titles published by Wolfe Medical Publications Ltd, please write to the
publishers at: Wolfe House, 3 Conway Street, London W1P 6HE, England.

General Editor, Wolfe Medical Atlases: G. Barry Carruthers, MD(London)

Contents

To our patients and colleagues

Acknowledgements

We wish to thank our colleagues for all their encouragement and advice in the production of this atlas.

Histopathology: Dr. A.C. Branfoot, Dr. J.N. Harcourt-Webster, Professor Kristin Henry.

Medical microbiology: Dr. R.E. Evans, Miss Jenny Midgely, Dr. D.C. Shanson.

Cytology: Dr. O.A.N. Husain.

And our clinical colleagues Dr. B.G. Gazzard, Dr. A.G. Lawrence, Dr. R.H. Phillips, Dr. J. Collins, and Professor C. Wastell.

Our thanks also to Dr Kwesi Tsiquaye (London School of Hygiene) and Dr Jonathan Weber (National Cancer Institute) for providing material.

We would like to pay tribute to the nursing, technical and administrative staff of our hospitals, for their devoted care and attention to our patients.

Our special thanks go to Miss Kath Meikle for typing the text.

We acknowledge the following for photographs:

E.M. Department, London School of Hygiene (**8,9**)

Professor Kristin Henry (**88, 139, 140**)

Professor A. Guz (**99**)

A. Boyleston (**105**)

I. Murray-Lyon (**131, 135**)

P.G. Elliott (**138**)

Miss G. Midgely (**164**)

A.G. Lawrence (**193**)

Part 1   The AIDS epidemic

Section 1: Epidemiology

Acquired immunodeficiency syndrome (AIDS) was first recognised in Los Angeles and New York in 1981 with an extraordinary outbreak of Pneumocystis carinii pneumonia and Kaposi's sarcoma in previously fit young men. Before this date both conditions had been very rare. Previously, Pneumocystis carinii pneumonia had been confined to those immunocompromised by age, known malignant disease or immunosuppressive therapy. Kaposi's sarcoma had been seen usually in those of Jewish and Mediterranean extraction. The new cases were found to be occurring in special risk groups, suggesting that a single infection with a blood- and semen-borne virus, like the Hepatitis B virus, might be responsible.

Table 1

Risk groups		
	Homosexual	72%
	Intravenous drug abusers	17%
	Haitian	4%
	Haemophiliacs	1%
	Blood transfusion recipients	1%
	Heterosexual partners	1%
	Unclassified	4%

Soon, other opportunistic infections were described in the same risk groups:

Table 2

Protozoa	*Virus*	
Pneumocystis carinii	Cytomegalovirus	
Toxoplasma gondii	Herpes simplex	(The herpes group)
Cryptosporidia	Herpes zoster	
	Epstein-Barr	
Fungi	*Bacteria*	
Candida albicans	Atypical mycobacteria	
Cryptococcus neoformans		

The unusual bias towards protozoal, fungal and viral organisms suggested a defect of cell mediated immunity.

THE DEFINITION OF AIDS (As defined for reporting purposes by the Center for Disease Control (CDC), Atlanta, Georgia, USA)

The occurrence of a *reliably diagnosed* disease that is at least moderately indicative of an underlying cellular immune deficiency in a patient with no other known underlying cause other than HTLV III/LAV infection for such, nor any other cause of reduced resistence reported to be associated with that disease.

Diseases at least moderately indicative of an underlying cellular immune deficiency include:

Protozoal
Pneumocystis carinii pneumonia
Toxoplasmosis – pneumonia or CNS
Cryptosporidiosis and Isosporiasis – diarrhoea over one month
Stronglyoidosis – pneumonia, CNS or disseminated

Fungal
Candidiasis – oesophageal or bronchopulmonary
Cryptococcus – pulmonary, CNS or disseminated
Histoplasmosis – disseminated
Aspergillosis – CNS or disseminated

Viral
Cytomegalovirus – pulmonary, gut or CNS
Herpes simplex virus – severe mucocutaneous disease for over one month, pulmonary, gut or disseminated
Progressive multifocal leukoencephalopathy

Bacterial
Atypical Mycobacteriosis – disseminated (species other than M. Tuberculosis, or M. lepra)

Cancer
Kaposi's sarcoma – no age restriction
Cerebral lymphoma
Non-Hodgkin's lymphoma – diffuse, undifferentiated and of B cell or unknown phenotype
Lymphoreticular malignancy – more than three months after an opportunistic infection

Other
Chronic lymphoid interstitial pneumonitis in children under 13 years

Note Patients are excluded if they have a negative result on testing for serum antibody to HTLV III/LAV, have no other type of HTLV III/LAV test with a positive result and do not have a low number of T-helper lymphocytes or a low ratio of T-helper to T-suppressor lymphocytes. In the absence of test results patients satisfying all other criteria are included.

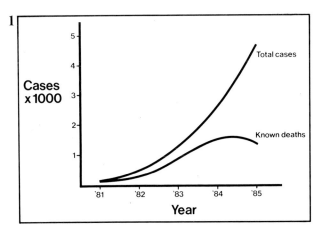

Cases x 1000

Total cases

Known deaths

Year

1 The extraordinary exponential rise in numbers of cases of AIDS in the USA since 1981. This rise with a doubling in the rate of cases every six to twelve months is now being repeated in many countries worldwide. Note that mortality is high. It approaches 100% after three years.

Section 2: Immunology

Immunological investigation of patients with AIDS revealed the defect in cell mediated immunity that the pattern of opportunistic infections suggested. Three particular abnormalities on immune function testing were found to be occurring together in an unusual and distinctive combination that has come to be known as the *AIDS triad:*

N.B

1 Decreased numbers of helper T lymphocytes, (often leading to a decreased T-helper/T-suppressor ratio and/or to an absolute lymphopaenia).
2 Hypergammaglobulinaemia. (↑ IgG) cause ?
3 Impaired response to recall antigens on skin testing.

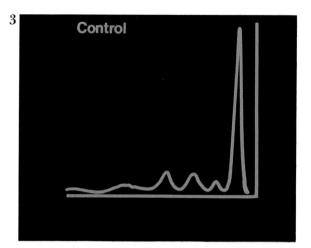

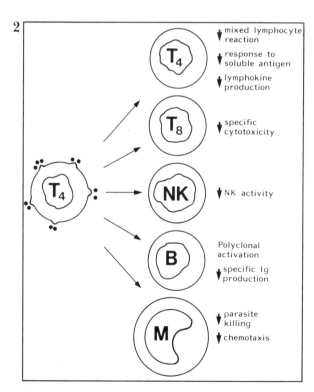

2 **The T-helper lymphocyte** has been described as the conductor of the immunological orchestra and certainly it influences the function of many other cells in the immune system, including B lymphocyte and macrophage function as shown. Most defects in immune function described in AIDS can be explained by a decrease in T-helper lymphocyte function.

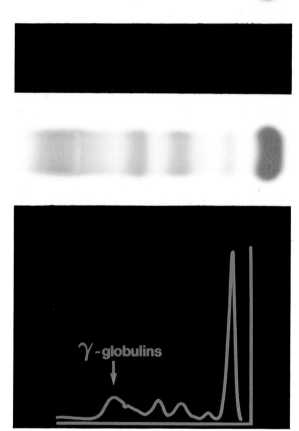

3 Serum protein electrophoretic strip in a patient with AIDS showing a polyclonal rise in gammaglobulins. This rise is usually largely due to IgG. The cause of the increased immunoglobulin production is uncertain.

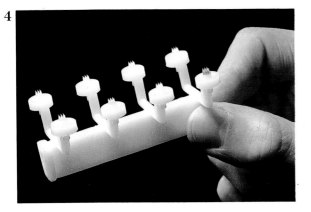

4 **A multiple applicator*** for delayed-type hypersensitivity skin testing, which tests for tetanus, diphtheria, streptococcus, tuberculin, candida, trichophyton, proteus and has a control head.

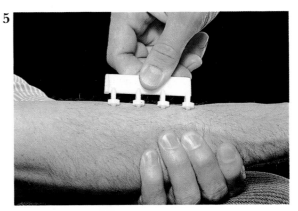

5 **Application to forearm.**

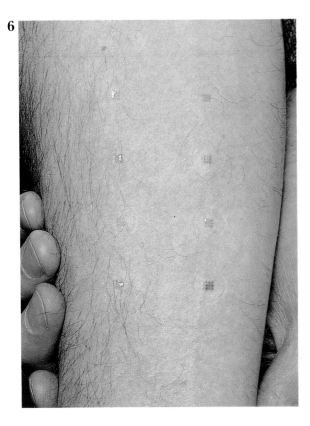

6 Forearm showing imprint immediately after application.

*Multitest CMI by Merieux UK Limited

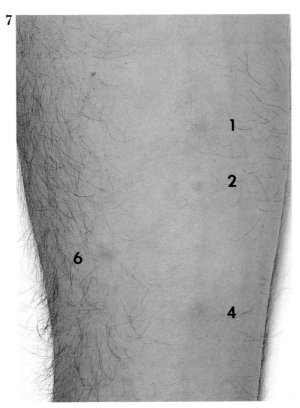

7 Same forearm showing normal response to tetanus (1), diphtheria (2), tuberculin (4) and candida (6) at 48 hours. A lesser response is usually seen in patients with AIDS.

Section 3: Virology

In 1983 Barre-Sinoussi and colleagues in Paris isolated a retrovirus from a patient with lymphadenopathy. They named the virus Lymphadenopathy Associated Virus (LAV). In 1984 Gallo and colleagues in the USA isolated a retrovirus they termed Human T-cell Lymphotropic Virus type III (HTLV III) from several patients with AIDS. These two isolates have subsequently been found to be identical, and are now recognised to be the cause of AIDS. The virus is now termed HTLV III/LAV or Human Immunodeficiency Virus (HIV).

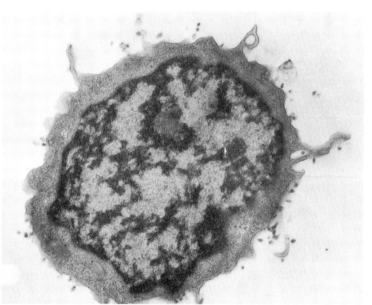

8 **A malignant T-lymphocyte** growing in cell culture showing budding of HTLV III/LAV virions from the cell surface. HTLV III/LAV is difficult to maintain in cell culture unless rapidly growing malignant T-cells are used. Ordinary T-lymphocyte cell cultures are rapidly killed off by HTLV III/LAV.

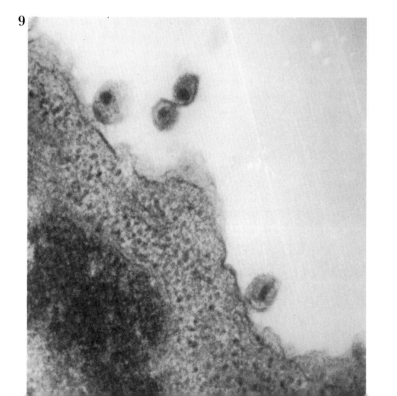

9 **Close-up of HTLV III/LAV virions budding from the cell surface.** The cylindrical protein core of the virus can be seen both in longitudinal and cross-section, surrounded by a glycoprotein outer membrane.

Retroviruses are RNA viruses, their name referring to the fact that RNA transcription proceeds in a reverse direction (RNA to DNA) before the viral genome can be incorporated into the host genome and viral replication commence. This essential retrograde step is dependent upon the presence of a viral enzyme called reverse transcriptase. Pharmocological inhibition of this enzyme is currently being explored as a method of controlling HTLV III/LAV.

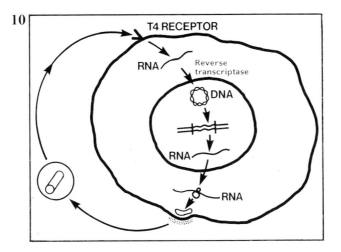

10 Diagrammatic representation of retrovirus replication.

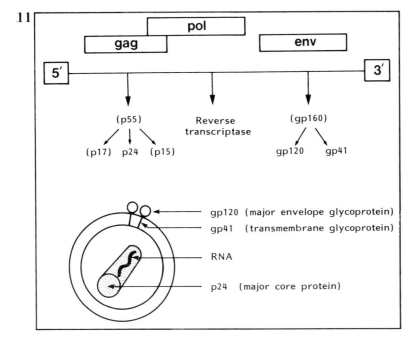

11 Schematic representation of the genome of HTLV III/LAV. Three principal genes code for the group associated antigen (gag), the reverse transcriptase or polymerase (pol), and the envelope glycoproteins (env). The principal core protein is of molecular weight 24,000 (p24). The principal envelope glycoproteins are of molecular weight 41,000 and 120,000 (gp41 and gp120). Precursor proteins of molecular weight 55,000 and 160,000 (p55 and gp160) are formed in infected cells, but are not present in intact virus particles.

Section 4: The HTLV III antibody test

Over 95% of patients infected with HTLV III/ LAV can be shown to have circulating antibodies to viral proteins. A small number of patients have been demonstrated to be infected with virus, by virus isolation techniques, and yet are seronegative. Thus, if clinical signs and symptoms suggestive of HTLV III/LAV disease are present but the test is negative, a clinician should not necessarily dismiss the diagnosis. Most patients probably seroconvert within a month of infection. However, some seronegative patients with symptoms and signs of disease may become positive months or years after infection (see **123**).

It is now generally believed that any patient seropositive for HTLV III/LAV antibodies remains infected and infectious for life. This is in contradistinction to Hepatitis B when the presence of antibodies means that the patient is no longer infectious. HTLV III/LAV may be isolated from greater than 80% of seropositive individuals up to six years after infection, and related animal retroviruses consistently result in persisting infection.

Several different methods for detecting HTLV III/LAV antibodies are now available (see below).

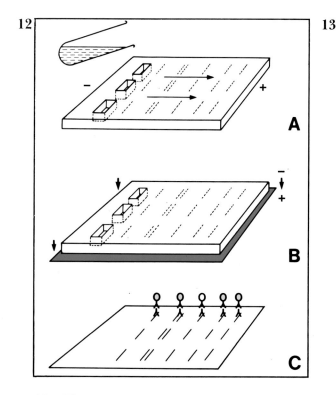

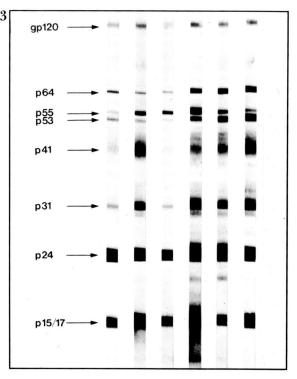

12 The Western blot method involves electrophoresis of disrupted HTLV III/LAV virions on slab gels. Most viral antigens can thus be individually detected. Cells of a malignant T-cell line infected with HTLV III/LAV are lysed and the lysate centrifuged and placed in wells on a polyacrylomide gel slab (A). Electrophoresis then separates the various viral proteins by molecular weight and charge. When this is complete the slab gel is placed adjacent to a nitrocellulose sheet and the viral proteins 'blotted' upon it again using electrophoresis (B). The patient's serum is then added to the nitrocellulose sheet and, if HTLV III/ LAV antibodies are present they will react with the viral antigens. After washing, labelled antihuman immunoglobulin is then applied and the 'Western blot' of the viral proteins is visualised (C). The Western blot is one of the most reliable forms of HTLV III/LAV antibody testing. As with all forms of antibody testing, however, very occasional false positive or false negative results may be obtained. In view of this, a result should probably always be confirmed by a repeat test using a different method – especially if the patient does not have clear symptoms and signs of HTLV III/LAV disease.

13 Western blot results. Note several viral proteins and glycoproteins are represented (see **11**).

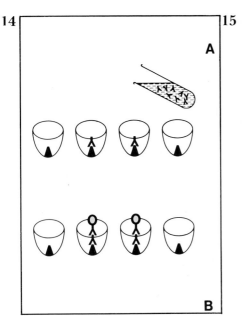

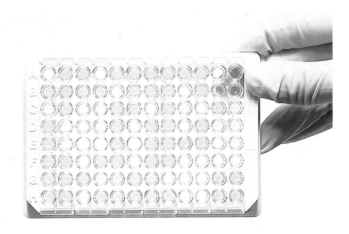

they bind to the antigen. After washing, labelled antihuman immunoglobulin is added and a visible reaction occurs if HTLV III/LAV antibodies are present.

14   The ELISA Test (Enzyme Linked Immuno-Sorbent Assay). The ELISA test is relatively simple and easy to perform. HTLV III/LAV infected malignant T-cells are lysed and fixed to the base of wells on a test plate. All the viral antigens are thus represented and not separated as in the Western blot test. The patient's serum is added to the wells and if antibodies are present

15   ELISA wells showing positive and negative test results.

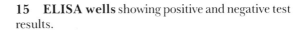

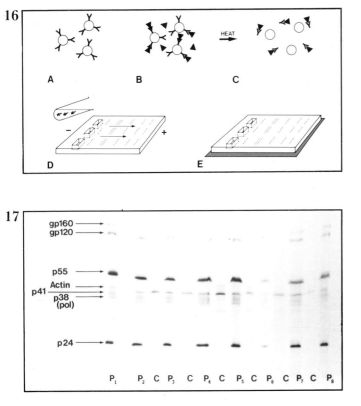

16   The RIPA Test (Radio Immune Precipitin Assay). This third form of HTLV III/LAV antibody testing is also highly reliable. The patient's serum is added to protein coated plastic beads and any immunoglobulin molecules present bind to the surface of the beads (A). Radioactive HTLV III/LAV infected malignant T-cell lysate (prepared by adding labelled methionine to cell culture) is added. Labelled HTLV III/LAV antigen binds to HTLV III/LAV antibody if present on the surface of the beads (B). Heat is then used to separate the antigen antibody complexes from the surface of the beads (C). The complexes are then separated by electrophoresis in polyacrylamide gel (D). When this is complete the gel, with the separated radioactive viral antigens, is placed against an x-ray plate and the RIPA result made visible (E).

17   Photograph of an x-ray plate of a RIPA result. Note that the line representing actin represents a cellular protein from the malignant T-cell line and not a viral component. It can be seen to be present in control sera as well as patients' sera.

Section 5: Origin of the AIDS virus

HTLV III/LAV seems likely to have originated in central Africa where serum samples from the early 1970s have been found to show a high incidence of seropositivity. No serum samples stored in the United States prior to 1978 have been found to be seropositive. Although HTLV III/LAV appears to have been present in Africa longer than in the United States the rising incidence of cases in Africa suggests a new epidemic.

Cases were recorded in Haiti before the USA, and this may have been due to the fact that migrant Haitian workers spent periods of time in central Africa in the 1960s and 1970s, and some returned to their homeland. In the 1970s Haiti was popular as a holiday resort for homosexual men from the USA. Many patients in Europe and Australasia appear to have contracted their infection in the USA. HTLV III/LAV is now epidemic worldwide.

In the western world the vast majority of cases are seen in homosexual men, but in Africa both sexes are equally affected. This, as well as cases after artificial insemination, suggests that the virus is easily transmitted by vaginal as well as anal intercourse.

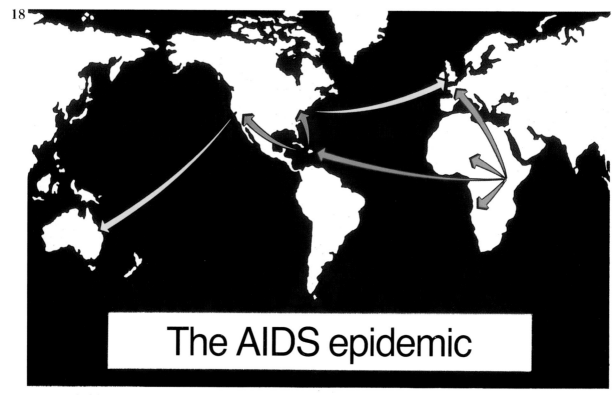

The AIDS epidemic

18   Probable origin and spread of the AIDS
virus – worldwide.

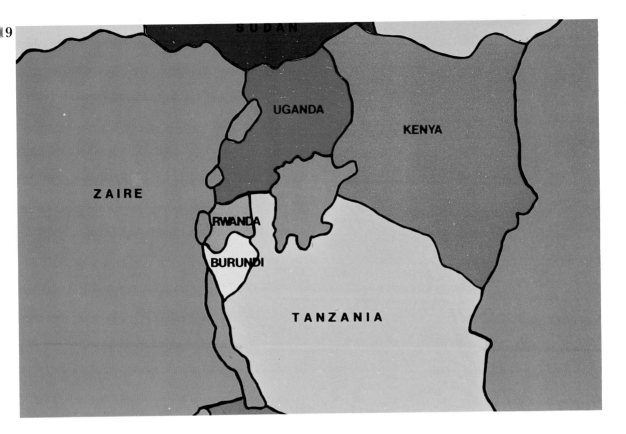

19 Map of central Africa showing countries of highest incidence of HTLV III/LAV disease – Ruanda, Burundi and southern Uganda. In these countries the epidemic is known locally as 'SLIM disease'.

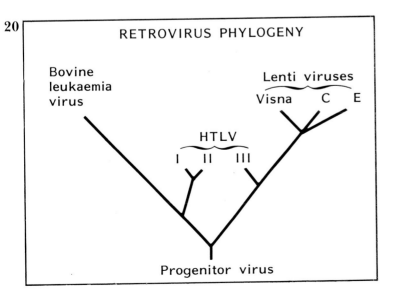

20 The phylogeny of HTLV III/LAV. Interestingly, the HTLV III/LAV genome is more closely related to that of the lenti viruses than to that of the other described Human T-cell Lymphotropic Viruses (type I and type II). The lenti viruses cause degenerative brain disease in sheep and goats, similar to some of the central nervous system disease seen in AIDS. HTLV I causes human T-cell leukaemia. HTLV II is not known to cause disease in man.

Section 6: Clinical spectrum of HTLV III/LAV disease

It is now realised that so far the syndrome of AIDS is seen in only a small proportion of those infected by HTLV III/LAV. Other clinical syndromes have been defined:

Definitions

1   AIDS (see page 9)

2   AIDS related complex (ARC)

Two Clinical findings plus *Two Laboratory* abnormalities

- Fatigue
- Night sweats
- Lymphadenopathy ≥ 3 months
- Weight loss (>10% total body weight)
- Fever > 3 months
- Diarrhoea

- Decreased T-helper cell count
- Increased serum globulins
- Anergy

3   Persistent generalised lymphadenopathy (PGL)

  (i) Lymphadenopathy of at least three months duration involving two or more extrainguinal sites.
  (ii) Absence of any current illness or drug use known to cause lymphadenopathy.
(iii) Presence of reactive hyperplasia in a lymph node if a biopsy is performed.

At any given time only a proportion of those infected with HTLV III/LAV have AIDS, or one of the other syndromes.

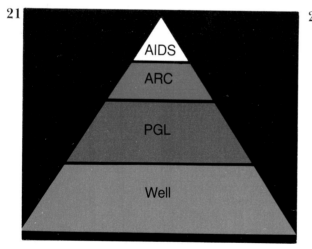

21   The total population of those infected with HTLV III/LAV. A small proportion have AIDS, a larger proportion suffer from various manifestations of the AIDS related complex (ARC) and an even larger proportion are well but for the presence of persistent generalised lymphadenopathy (PGL). In many there are no symptoms or signs of infection.

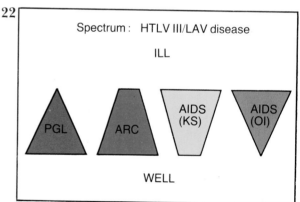

22   Proportions of patients in the various subgroups who are either ill or well. Note that most patients with AIDS defined by the occurrence of opportunistic infection, are ill, but that quite a large proportion of patients with AIDS, as defined by Kaposi's Sarcoma, are well. Many patients with ARC are as unwell as patients with AIDS. The diagram illustrates the considerable overlap in clinical condition between these relatively arbitrarily defined syndromes.

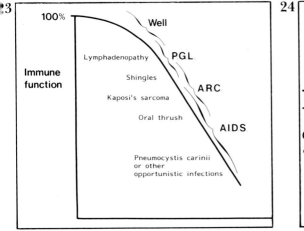

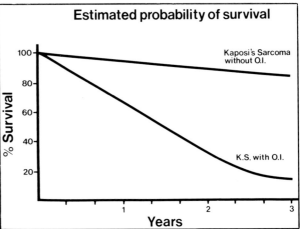

23 The relationship of immune function to the various defined syndromes. Note again the considerable overlap.

24 Survival curves in patients with Kaposi's sarcoma with and without opportunistic infections. A considerable proportion of patients with Kaposi's sarcoma without opportunistic infection survive for prolonged periods. The development of an opportunistic infection is thus more ominous than the development of uncomplicated Kaposi's sarcoma.

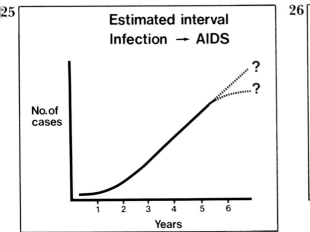

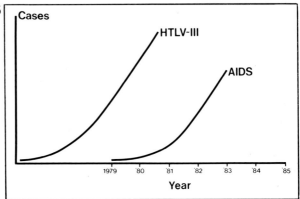

25 Incubation period. The interval between infection with HTLV III/LAV to development of AIDS is very variable. Following contaminated blood transfusion the incubation period has been recorded to vary from eight months to six years. For the six years that the epidemic has been followed a constant proportion of infected individuals have developed AIDS each year after infection. It is not yet certain whether a constant proportion of infected individuals will continue to develop AIDS every year, or whether this proportion will tail off to give an average incubation of four to six years (as indicated by the dotted lines). Until the

incubation period is more precisely defined it is not possible to know what percentage of those infected will eventually develop AIDS. To date some 10% of those who have been carrying the virus for five to six years have developed AIDS, and a further 25% have developed ARC. These percentages may rise.

26 Incubation period of AIDS, indicating the spread of HTLV III/LAV through a community precedes the spread of clinical AIDS by several years. This has serious social implications in that HTLV III/LAV may spread widely within a community before disease is apparent and precautions are taken.

Part 2 Clinical manifestations of AIDS

Clinical presentation of AIDS

AIDS may present in many different ways:

1 **Pneumonia**
2 **Kaposi's sarcoma**
3 **Central nervous sytem disease**
4 **Gastrointestinal disease**
5 **Lymphoma**
6 **Pyrexia of unknown origin (PUO)**

Section 7: Pneumonia

Some 60% of patients with AIDS present with pneumonia, the vast majority of which is caused by the protozoan, Pneumocystis carinii. A typical patient presents with a persistent non-productive dry cough of some weeks duration, (which comes in paroxysms and may lead to vomiting), exertional dyspnoea and fever. The most important clinical sign is tachypnoea at rest. Other clinical signs in the chest are usually absent. A blood gas analysis may show hypoxia, and a chest x-ray may show bilateral interstitial shadowing. However, any or all of these investigations may be normal.

Fibreoptic bronchoscopy with alveolar lavage and/or transbronchial biopsy is usually required to establish the diagnosis. Sometimes sputum induced by hypertonic saline inhalation may contain pneumocysts.

TACHYPNEA AT REST

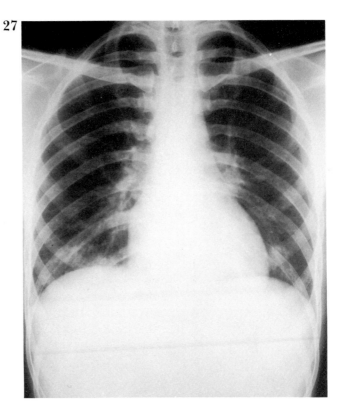

27 Pneumocystis carinii pneumonia (PCP) on presentation. Although the chest x-ray shows little shadowing, the patient was markedly hypoxic on admission and a transbronchial biopsy revealed Pneumocystis carinii.

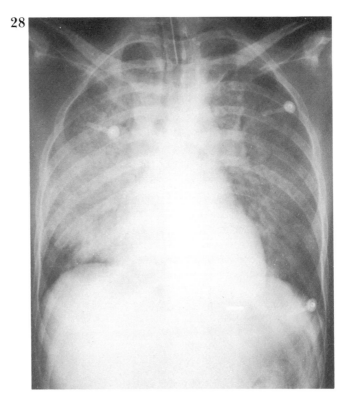

28 The same patient four days later showing rapid deterioration. This patient died despite high dose intravenous co-trimoxazole – the treatment of choice.

29

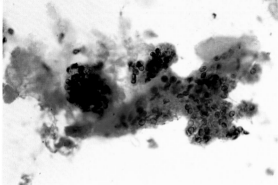

29   Cytological preparation of numerous Pneumocystis carinii from bronchial washings. (Silver methenamine – Grocott ×160).

30

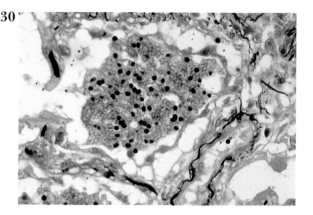

30   Pneumocystis carinii. Transbronchial biopsy of lung stained by Grocott method to show Pneumocystitis carinii in the intra-alveolar exudate. (Grocott ×100).

31

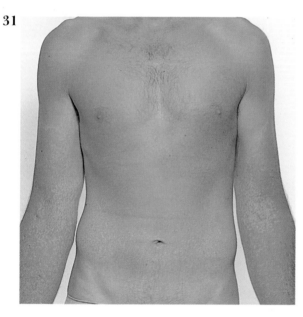

32

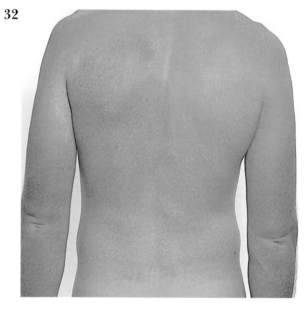

31 and 32   Co-trimoxazole rash in patient with Pneumocystis carinii pneumonia. Hypersensitivity to co-trimoxazole is very common in AIDS patients and occurs in 40 to 60%. A febrile reaction is also common. An alternative treatment is pentamidine by injection. Both drugs are equally effective and a change from one to the other or simultaneous administration is seldom of benefit.

Low dose co-trimoxazole is frequently used as an effective prophylaxis against recurrence of PCP. An alternative is weekly sulfadoxine-pyrimethamine (Fansidar).

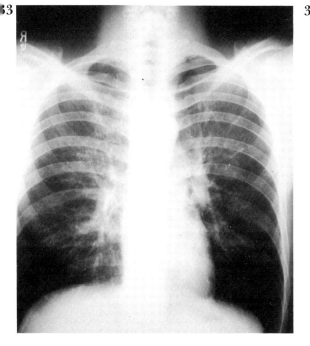

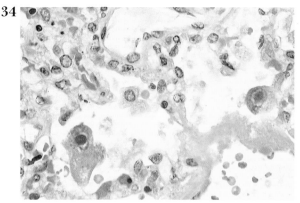

33 CMV pneumonitis, the next most common pulmonary pathogen in AIDS. The clinical presentation is indistinguishable from PCP, and in fact mixed infections often occur. Treatment is now available with 2 dihydroxy 6 propoxymethyl guanine (DHPG) or phosphonoformate (Foscarnet). In a mixed infection treatment of PCP alone may result in recovery.

34 CMV inclusion bodies in alveolar wall. (Transbronchial biopsy) (H & E ×160)

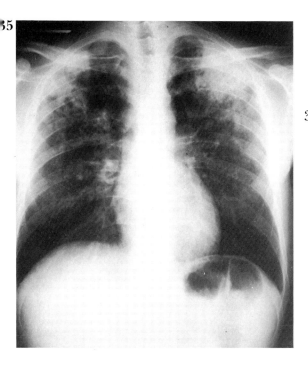

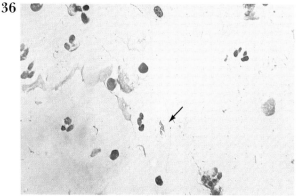

36 Sputum showing acid-alcohol fast organisms (Ziehl-Nielson stain) amidst leucocytes (×160). Patients with PCP and CMV pneumonitis usually do not produce sputum, unlike tuberculosis where a productive cough is usual and a diagnosis may be made more easily by investigation of the sputum.

Mycobacterium tuberculosis in these patients usually responds promptly to conventional antituberculous agents. Atypical mycobacteria, most commonly Mycobacterium avium-intracellulare, responds poorly to the usual antituberculous drugs, but ansamycin or clofazimine may be helpful.

35 Patient with pulmonary tuberculosis. Tuberculosis is more common in patients with HTLV III/LAV disease. Infection with atypical mycobacteria defines a patient as having AIDS. Because M. tuberculosis is not confined to the immunocompromised a patient with this infection who is seropositive to HTLV III/LAV would be defined as having ARC or 'lesser AIDS'.

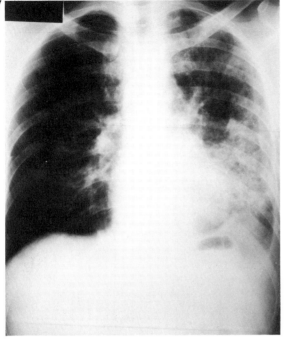

37 **Patient with toxoplasma pneumonia,** a rare opportunist infection in the lung even in AIDS.

38 **The same patient as 37 showing toxoplasma trophozoites** (transbronchial biopsy). (Grocott ×400).

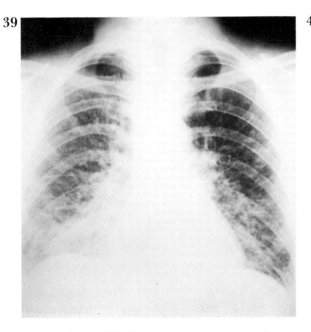

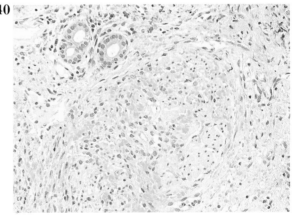

39 **Patient with Kaposi's sarcoma involving the lung.** Note that the interstitial shadowing is very similar to that seen in PCP and CMV pneumonitis. Usually the onset of symptoms in patients with pulmonary Kaposi's sarcoma is more gradual without fever or cough. However, occasionally symptoms develop rapidly and mimic AIDS pneumonia.

40 Bronchial biopsy showing Kaposi's sarcoma (H&E ×60). Note the multiple irregular-shaped vascular spaces lined by pleomorphic endothelial cells with extravasated erythrocytes (see also 87). The diagnosis may be suspected at bronchoscopy when haemorrhagic lesions are seen.

The prognosis of Kaposi lung is grave. There may be transient improvement with systemic chemotherapy, but patients do poorly with radiotherapy.

41

42

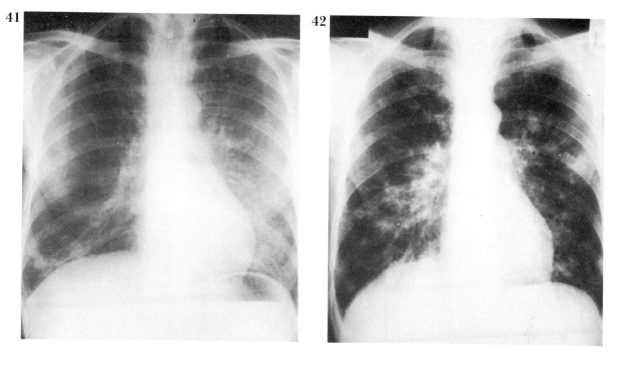

41 Interstitial shadowing in both lung fields in patient with Pneumocystis carinii pneumonia.

42 Same patient as **41** seven months later after successful treatment of PCP, but now, with the development of Kaposi's sarcoma of the lung. Note different appearance of the pulmonary shadowing in these two different conditions.

43

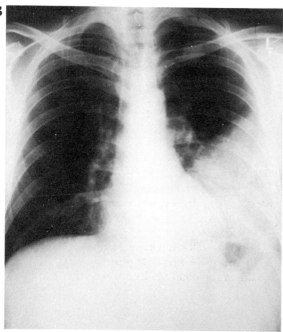

43 Patient with pneumococcal lobar pneumonia. Lobar pneumonia due to Pneumococcus and Haemophilus appears to be more common in patients with HTLV III/LAV disease. These infections, however, can occur in the non-immunocompromised host and thus a seropositive patient with lobar pneumonia would be classified as having only ARC or 'lesser AIDS'.

Section 8: Kaposi's sarcoma

Kaposi's sarcoma is a vascular tumour, previously seen largely in elderly patients of Mediterranean and Jewish stock. It is now the second commonest presentation of AIDS after pneumonia. The presentation of 'classical' Kaposi's sarcoma is on the lower limb, and is only very slowly progressive in most patients. A similar distribution on the lower limbs may be seen in AIDS, but more commonly discrete vascular tumours are scattered widely over the body.

Interestingly, while Kaposi's sarcoma is common in homosexuals with AIDS, it is rare in other risk groups. The reason for this is unknown but it is widely believed that the sarcoma is secondary to an as yet unidentified 'opportunistic' virus widespread in the homosexual community but rare in others.

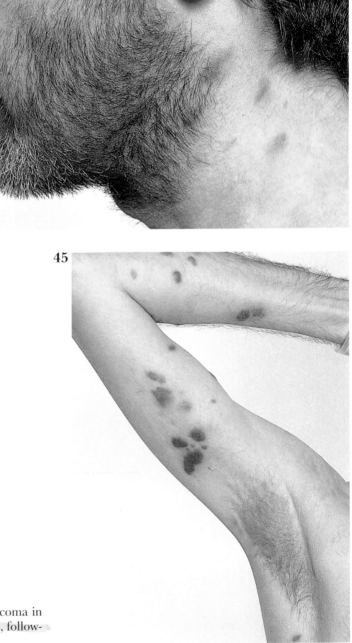

44 and **45** Typical lesions of Kaposi's sarcoma in patients with AIDS. Note linearity of lesions, following skin creases – a common appearance.

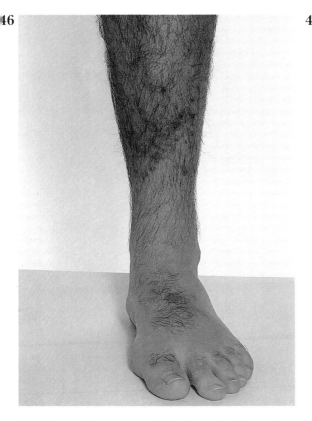

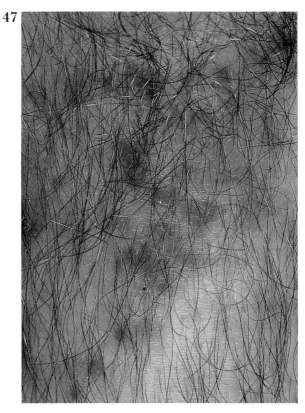

46 **Kaposi's sarcoma of the lower leg** in a patient with AIDS, showing a 'classical' distribution.

47 Close-up of the patient in **46**.

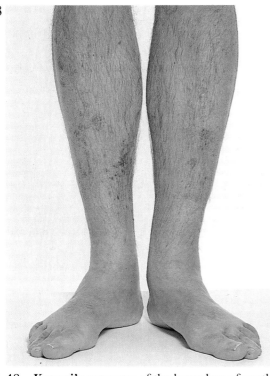

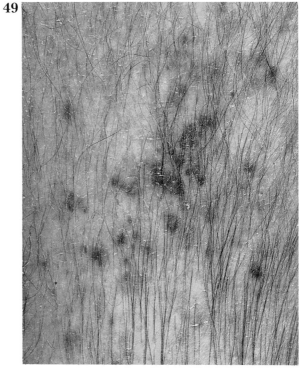

48 **Kaposi's sarcoma** of the lower legs of another patient with AIDS.

49 Close-up of the patient in **48**.

50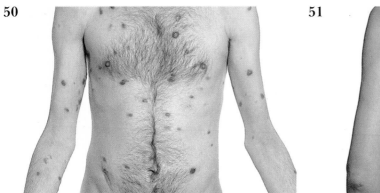

51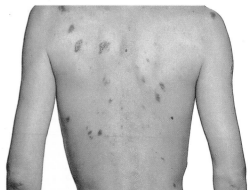

50 to **53** Widespread Kaposi's sarcoma in different patients with AIDS.

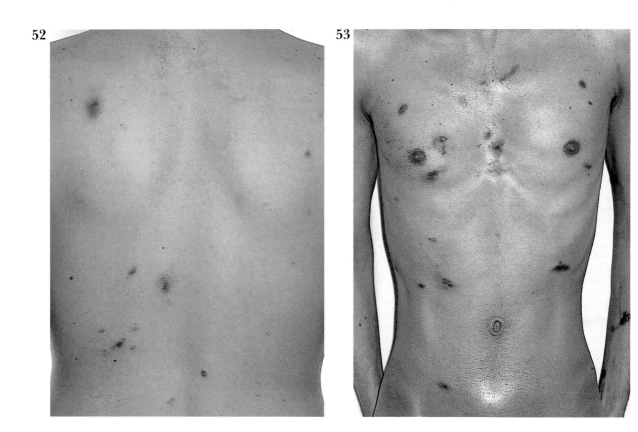

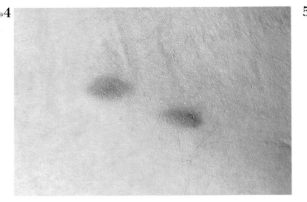

54 to **56**   Close-up of typical Kaposi's sarcoma in patients with AIDS.

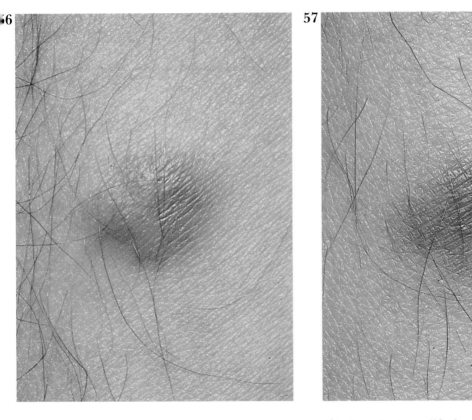

57   Same lesion as **56**, showing flattening and spontaneous regression of Kaposi's sarcoma over a six month period. Individual lesions frequently regress spontaneously. Rarely, all lesions may regress spontaneously.

58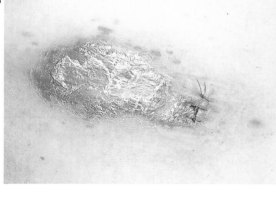

59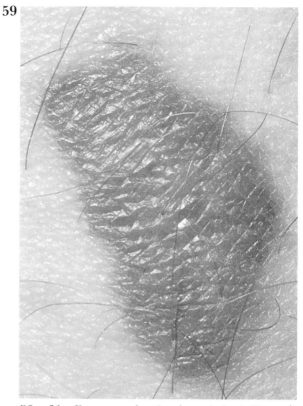

60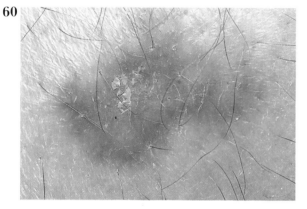

58 to **61**   Four cases showing the variation in Kaposi's sarcoma lesions. Note (**61**) that it can mimic malignant melanoma. Other lesions that may be confused with Kaposi's sarcoma are pyogenic granuloma and dermatofibroma.

61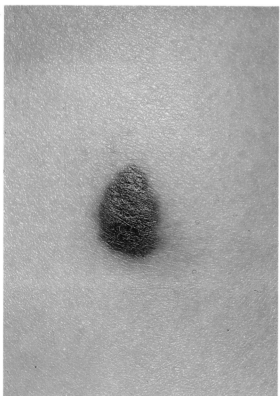

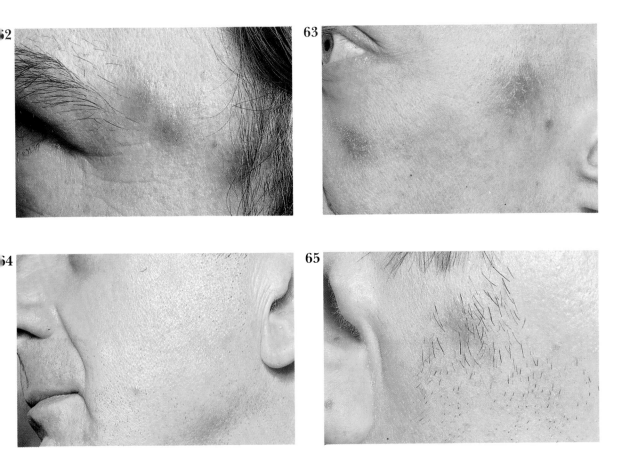

62 to **65**   Kaposi's sarcoma on the face.

66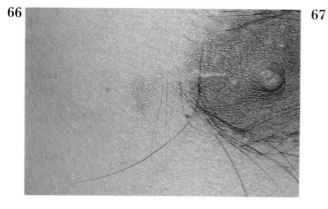

67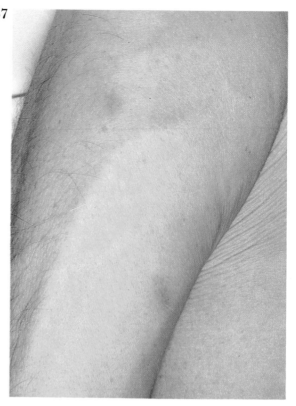

66 to **69** Early Kaposi's sarcoma lesions in patients with AIDS.

68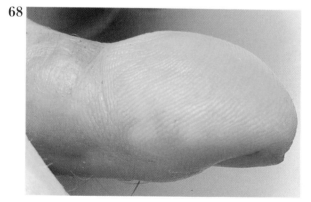

69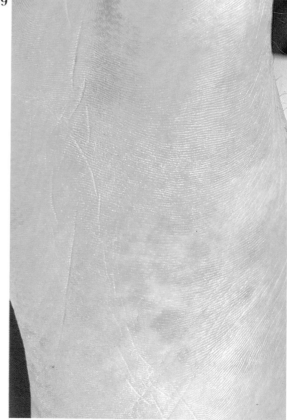

70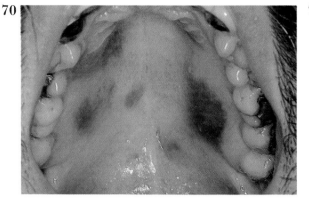

71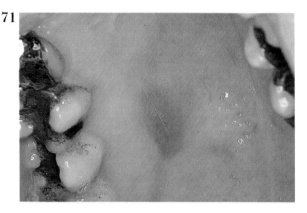

72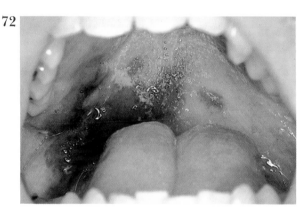

70 to 72   Kaposi's sarcoma lesions on palate in patients with AIDS. Note the lesions usually first appear on the hard palate just above the second molar teeth.

73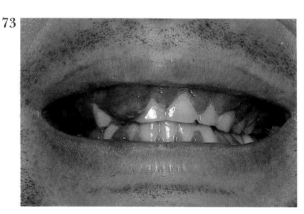

73   Kaposi's sarcoma of the gums simulating epulis. In this patient extensive involvement of the palate led to involvement of the gums. This patient's Kaposi's sarcoma was very aggressive and he died with pulmonary KS three months after presentation. Such a rapid progression is in fact unusual. Patients with KS are, in fact, more likely to die from an opportunistic infection than from extension of their tumour.

74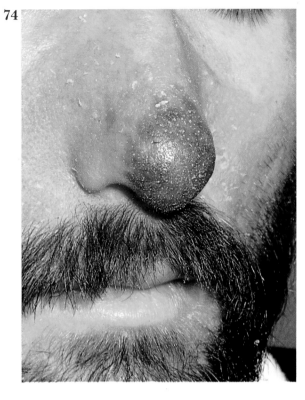

75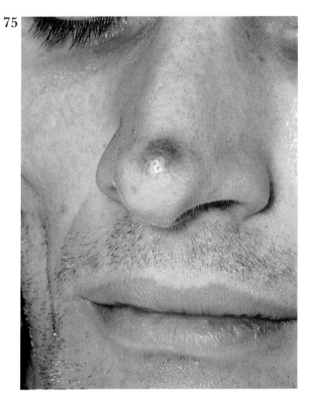

76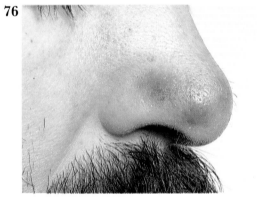

77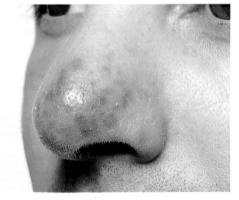

74 to **77** Kaposi's sarcoma frequently occurs on the tip of the nose.

78

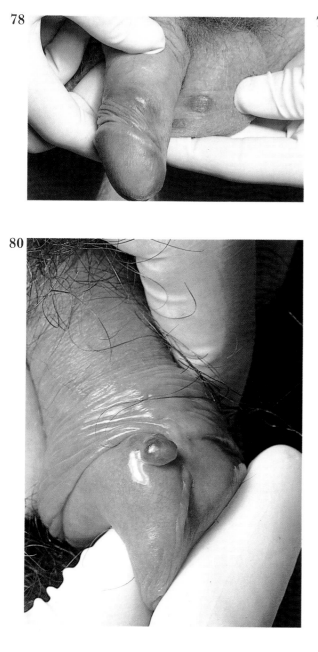

79

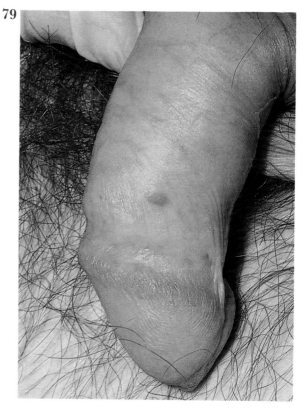

80

78 to **80** Kaposi's sarcoma lesions on the penis, another common site.

81 Kaposi's sarcoma favours the medial third of the lower eye lid as in this patient.

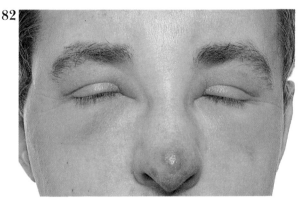

82 Periorbital oedema seen in this patient with Kaposi's sarcoma obstructing lymphatic drainage. (KS often involves lymph nodes and may be found on lymph node biopsy when there are no lesions on the skin. In such cases cutaneous KS may develop later.)

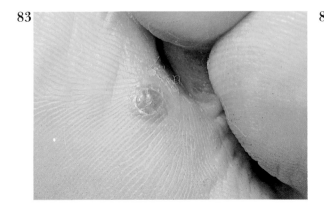

83 Kaposi's sarcoma lesions on the sole simulating pyogenic granuloma.

84 Same lesion as **83** two months later, showing progression.

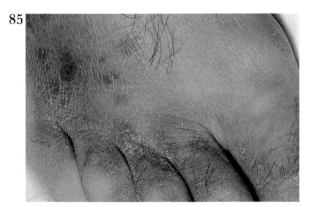

85 Kaposi's sarcoma on the dorsum of the foot – another appearance.

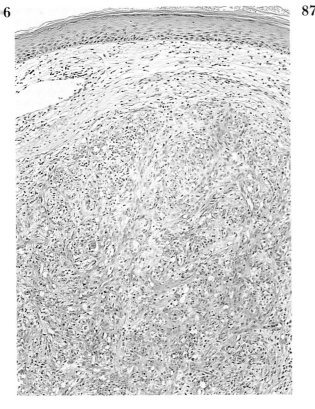

86 Skin with Kaposi's sarcoma (H & E ×25). Discrete intradermal nodule with vascular channels lined by atypical endothelial cells and copious extravasated erythrocytes with deposit of haemosiderin.

87 Higher magnification of **86** to show greatest detail and increased mitoses amongst atypical endothelial cells (H & E ×60).

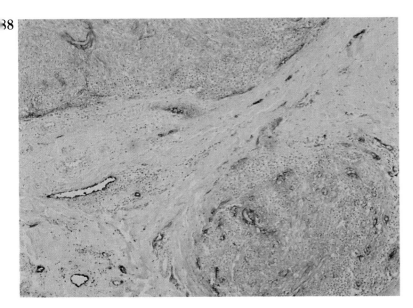

88 Immunocytochemical staining for Factor VIII. Both the normal endothelial and Kaposi sarcoma cells are positive suggesting that the latter are of endothelial origin.

Treatment of Kaposi's sarcoma

Kaposi's sarcoma responds to several different treatments:

1. Excision of individual lesions.
2. Radiotherapy – including electron beam therapy.
3. Chemotherapy – either intralesional or systemic.
4. Alpha-interferon.

Kaposi's sarcoma is rarely the direct cause of death, and treatment, even if successful, usually does not influence prognosis. Lesions are unsightly, however, and cosmetic and psychological benefit may accrue from treatment. If only one or two lesions are present, simple excision may be all that is required. A solitary large lesion, (e.g. **46**) is perhaps best treated with radiotherapy. Multiple small lesions can be treated by electron beam therapy or intralesional chemotherapy (0.1 ml of vinblastine 0.1-0.2 mg/ml every two weeks). Extensive disease may be treated by alpha interferon or systemic chemotherapy. Conventional combination chemotherapy regimes are immunosuppressive, and may worsen prognosis. Low dose single agent chemotherapy (e.g. vinblastine or VP16) is probably not significantly immunosuppressive. Alpha interferon, whilst safe, may have unpleasant side effects.

89
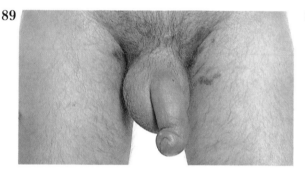

89 Oedema of genitalia in patient with Kaposi's sarcoma involving inguinal lymph nodes.

90

90 Resolution of oedema after radiotherapy treatment.

91
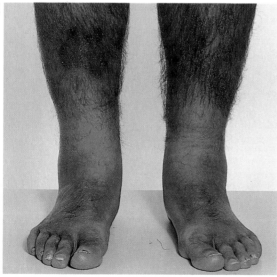

91 Kaposi's sarcoma of lower legs with oedema.

92
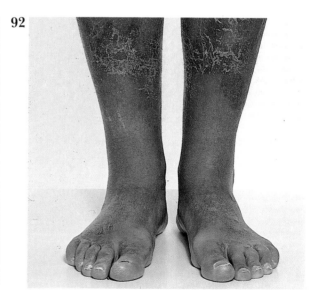

92 Same patient with resolution of oedema after radiotherapy to shins. Note also loss of hair.

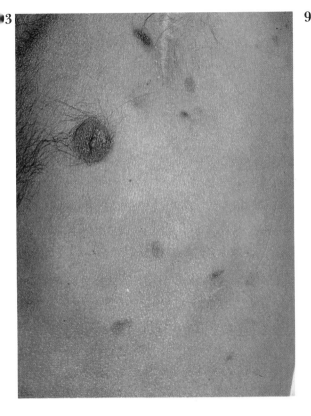

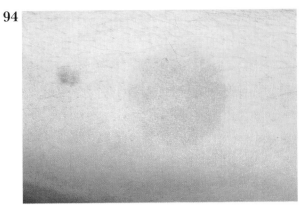

93 Kaposi's sarcoma on patient's flank after treatment with electron beam therapy. Note hyperpigmentation following treatment.

94 Kaposi's sarcoma lesion adjacent to site of lesion treated with electron beam (**93**). Treated lesion has resolved but hyperpigmentation remains.

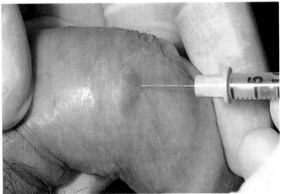

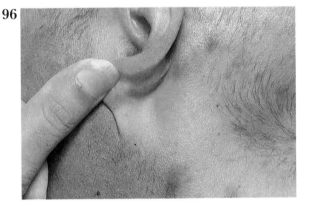

95 Lesion being injected with intralesional cytotoxic.

96 Patient showing phototoxic hyperpigmentation following VP16 systemic chemotherapy for Kaposi's sarcoma.

Section 9: Disease of the nervous system

Many opportunistic infections may involve the central nervous system in AIDS, and HTLV III/LAV may proliferate in the CNS.

CNS Presentation:

1 *Dementia*

　　Causes:　HTLV III/LAV CNS disease
　　　　　　　Cerebral lymphoma/cerebral
　　　　　　　gliosis
　　　　　　　Progressive multifocal
　　　　　　　leukoencephalopathy

2 *Meningitis*

　　Causes:　Cryptococcus
　　　　　　　Mycobacteria

3 *Focal lesions*

　　Causes:　Toxoplasma
　　　　　　　Fungal abscess

4 *Retinitis*

　　Cause:　CMV

5 *Myelopathy*

　　Cause:　HTLV III/LAV

It is important to note that the CNS presentation of AIDS is usually extremely subtle.

AIDS dementia is now a well recognised clinical entity. The initial presentation is minor short-term memory loss, but even when quite advanced it may be difficult to document with psychometric tests. HTLV III/LAV has been isolated frequently from CSF and is believed to be the cause.

Meningitis frequently presents with headache without neck stiffness and on lumbar puncture there may be no cells in the CSF. Organisms may be detected only if special stain techniques are performed (e.g. acid fast stain and India ink preparation) or after culture.

A raised CSF protein is common in both meningitis and dementia.

Focal lesions may lead to fitting.

Myelopathy may result in spastic paraparesis and urinary and faecal incontinence. Peripheral neuropathy may lead to foot drop. The likely cause is direct involvement of neural tissue with HTLV III/LAV.

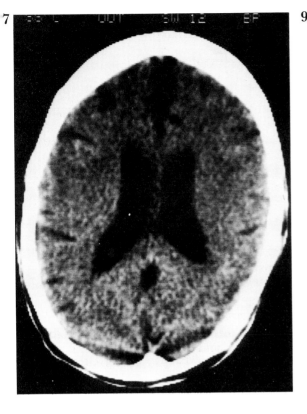

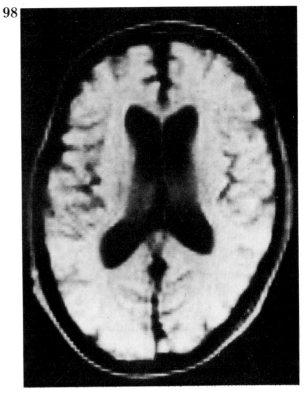

97 **Patient with AIDS dementia** showing cerebral atrophy with enlarged lateral ventricles.

98 NMR scan of previous patient showing shrunken cerebral hemispheres.

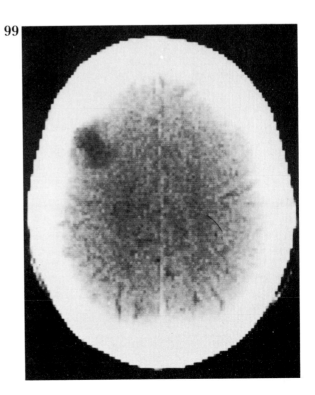

99 CT scan of patient with toxoplasma cerebral abscess.

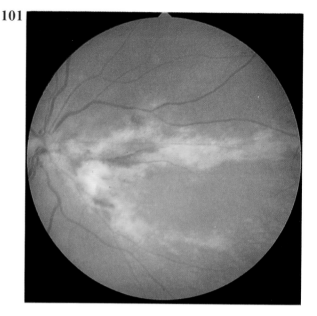

100 and **101** **CMV retinitis** in patient with AIDS. This serious opportunistic infection can rapidly progress to irreversible blindness. CMV causes a retinal vasculitis which leads to areas of infarction. Treatment is now available with DHPG or Foscarnet (see **33**), but maintenance therapy is required if reactivation is to be prevented.

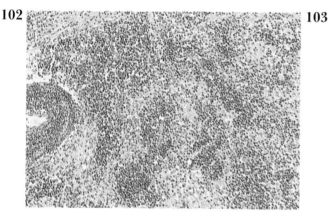

102 Brain from a patient with AIDS showing **microgliomatosis**, a form of malignant lymphoma. (H & E ×25) CNS lymphoma occurs with increased frequency in association with AIDS and recent evidence suggests that the causative agent is Epstein-Barr virus (EBV).

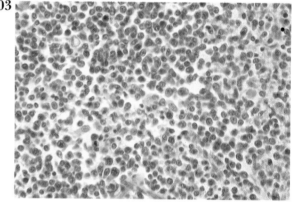

103 High power of **102**. Sheets of intermediate-sized cells having clefted nuclei, conspicuous nucleoli and fairly numerous mitotic figures (H & E ×100).

Section 10: Gastrointestinal disease

AIDS may present in the gastrointestinal system with either diarrhoea secondary to an opportunistic infection, oesophagitis, progressive anal herpes, or Kaposi's sarcoma of the gut.

Causes of diarrhoea that define AIDS:
1 Cryptosporidium
2 Cytomegalovirus (CMV)
3 Atypical mycobacteria

Cryptosporidium is a protozoal organism that was not known to be a pathogen in man before AIDS. It is now recognised as a common cause of travellers' diarrhoea, resulting in a one to two week illness in the non-immunocompromised host. In AIDS it can cause a severe chronic, even fatal, diarrhoea. It is important when investigating diarrhoea in HTLV III/LAV antibody positive patients, to look specifically for this parasite which is only visible with acid fast staining. Cryptosporidial diarrhoea may be treated with spiramycin, erythromycin, or clindamycin and quinine, but response is often unsatisfactory.

CMV causes a chronic diarrhoea often associated with abdominal pain and signs of peritonism. Rectal biopsy may reveal diagnostic inclusion bodies (**105**) but may often be negative. A relatively deep biopsy is required to show inclusion bodies. Treatment with DHPG or Foscarnet may be successful, but again maintenance therapy is usually required.

Atypical mycobacteria (especially Mycobacterium avium intracellulare) may involve the gastrointestinal tract extensively producing a Whipple's-like syndrome.

104 Cryptosporidium in a stool from a patient with diarrhoea. (Ziehl-Nielson ×160)

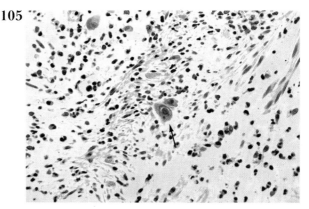

105 Cytomegalic inclusion body in the rectal mucosa of a patient with cytomegalovirus enterocolitis. Note the body surrounded by a clear halo and then the nuclear membrane. (H & E ×120)

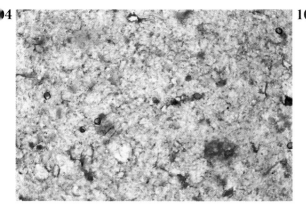

106 Mycobacterium avium intracellulare in stool. (Ziehl-Nielson ×160)

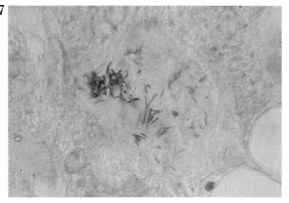

107 MAI in the liver of a patient with disseminated atypical mycobacterial infection.

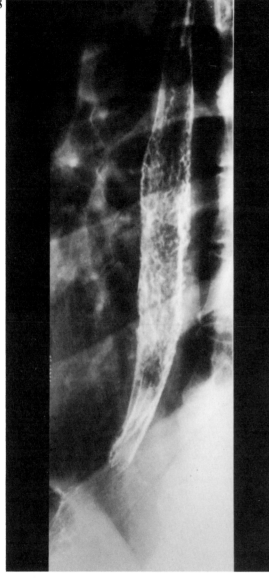

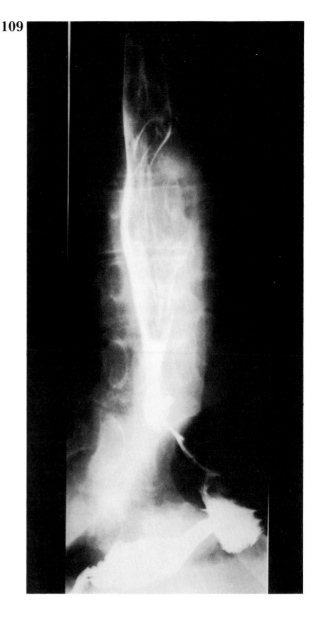

108 Candidal oesophagitis (barium swallow). The treatment of choice is ketoconazole. Dysphagia in HTLV III/LAV disease is most commonly due to candidal oesophagitis, but may be secondary to CMV or herpes simplex virus. The presence of candidal oesophagitis satisfies the CDC criteria for the diagnosis of AIDS.

109 Herpes simplex oesophagitis (barium swallow). This patient had a particularly painful dysphagia which responded promptly to intravenous acyclovir.

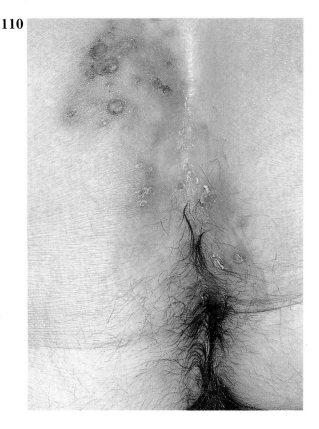

110 Progressive perianal herpes simplex.
Herpes simplex at the anus is an extremely common problem in patients with HTLV III/LAV disease, and when extensive this meets the CDC definition of AIDS. Very often only a tiny ulcer or fissure is seen, yet the patient may be in great discomfort. Treatment with oral acyclovir should not be delayed in patients with painful perianal lesions.

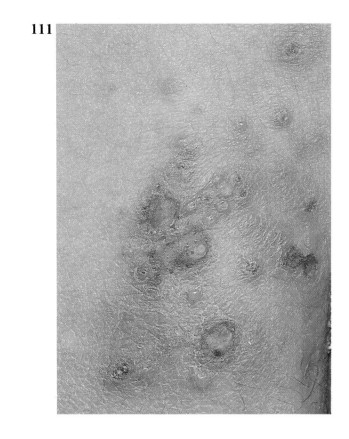

111 Close-up of patient in **110**.

Kaposi's sarcoma of the gastrointestinal tract

Kaposi's sarcoma frequently involves the gastrointestinal tract but it is usually asymptomatic. Lesions on the hard palate are common, and may be the site of presentation (**70** to **73**). Bowel obstruction occasionally occurs, haemorrhage is rare. The liver may be involved.

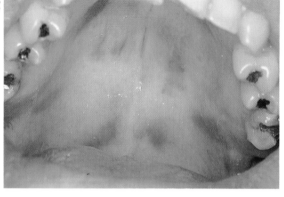

112 Kaposi's sarcoma of palate in patient with AIDS. (See also **70** to **73**).

113 Kaposi's sarcoma of uvula of patient with AIDS.

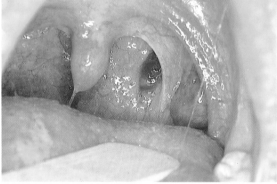

114 Kaposi's sarcoma of posterior pharyngeal wall.

115 Obstruction in rectum secondary to Kaposi's sarcoma (barium enema).

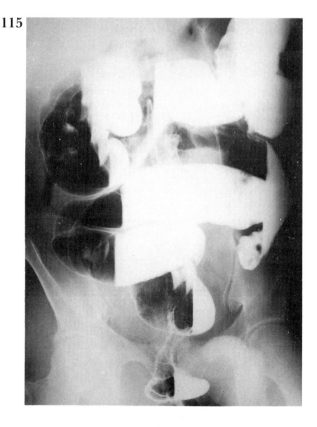

Other diarrhoeas

In HTLV III/LAV positive patients a wide range of organisms may cause diarrhoea. Such infections are not criteria enough for the CDC definition of AIDS, as they may cause diarrhoea in the non-immunocompromised. The protozoa giardia and entamoeba and the bacteria shigella and salmonella are common. These latter are intracellular bacterial parasites and require cell mediated immunity for their elimination. Although these infections respond to conventional treatment prolonged therapy is often required.

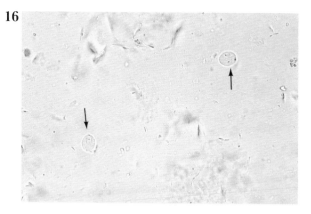

116 Giardia lamblia in the stool of patients with AIDS related complex (ARC). (Wet preparation ×160)

117 Shigella species culture growing from the stool of a patient with ARC and diarrhoea. (Xylose Lysine Desoxycholate agar – XLD). Note yellow lactose fermenting colonies of E. coli and colourless shigella species colonies.

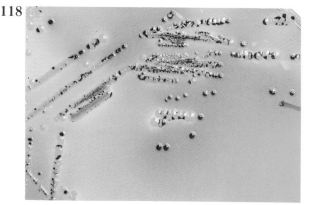

118 Salmonella typhimurium culture growing from the stool of a patient with ARC and gastroenteritis (XLD agar). Note yellow lactose fermenting colonies of E. coli and colourless colonies of salmonella with black centres and pink haloes.

Section 11: Lymphoma

The lymphoma of AIDS is usually of non-Hodgkin's type. It usually responds to conventional chemotherapy. However, the bone marrow is unusually susceptible to cytotoxic drugs, and the amount of treatment that can be given may be limited.

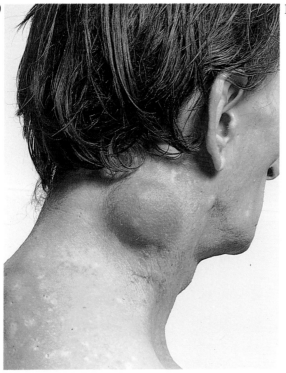

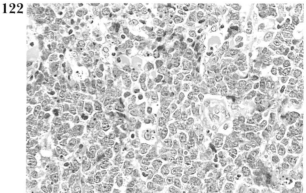

119 Posterior cervical lymph node enlarged secondary to lymphoma in patient with AIDS.

120 Lymph node biopsy from patient in **119**, showing non-Hodgkin's high grade histiocytic lymphoma (H & E ×100).

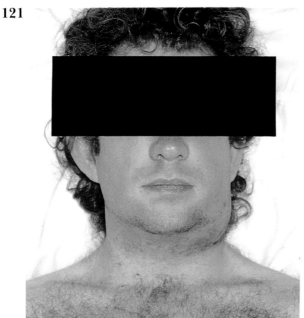

121 Enlarged anterior cervical nodes in patient with lymphoma.

122 Lymph node biopsy from patient in **121** showing poorly-differentiated diffuse non-Hodgkin's malignant lymphoma of small and intermediate cell type.

Section 12: Paediatric AIDS

AIDS in children shows some significant differences from the disease in adults. The incubation period is usually shorter and two clinical syndromes seen rarely in adult AIDS are common:

(i) Lymphocytic interstitial pneumonitis (LIP) – probably due to active Epstein-Barr virus infection, and

(ii) Chronic parotid swelling.

Also, gram negative septicaemia is a frequent cause of death, whereas this is seldom the case in adult AIDS.

It is important when considering the diagnosis of AIDS in children that every attempt be made to exclude a primary immunodeficiency disease. In a seronegative infant it is especially important to exclude deficiency of adenosine deaminase and purine nucleoside phosphorylase as deficiency of these enzymes can produce a syndrome reminiscent of AIDS.

Part 3 Clinical presentation of AIDS related complex

Patients with HTLV III/LAV disease more commonly present with one or more of the various manifestations of ARC than with AIDS itself. These are:

1 **Fatigue**
2 **Lymphadenopathy**
3 **Night sweats**
4 **Weight loss**
5 **Oral cavity disease**
6 **Skin disease**
7 **ENT problems**

Although the above are features of ARC, these clinical signs and symptoms are almost universal in AIDS patients. Many minor infections also occur and prompt treatment with antibiotics, antifungals or antivirals is desirable.

Section 13: Lymphadenopathy

Generalised lymphadenopathy that has persisted for more than three months in a homosexual patient is very likely to be due to HTLV III/LAV disease. It is so common a finding, that lymph node biopsy is no longer routine practice.

Biopsy is recommended if the patient has unusual constitutional symptoms, unusually large lymph nodes or is seronegative. This would exclude lymphoma or tuberculous adenitis. PGL is occasionally painful and may fluctuate. Often it regresses before the development of AIDS.

123   Visible lymph node in the neck of a patient with persistent generalised lymphadenopathy. Interestingly this patient had HTLV III/LAV seronegative PGL for three years, before seroconversion. He remains well after six years of PGL, but for the recent development of seborrhoeic dermatitis.

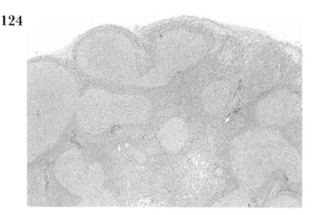

124   Lymph node with extensive follicular hyperplasia. This is the typical finding in PGL but is a nonspecific finding seen in many reactive lymphadenopathies. (H & E ×10).

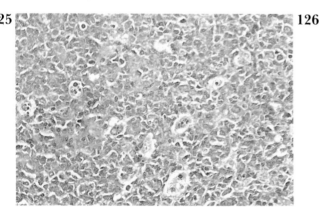

125   Higher power of reactive germinal centre in same node as **124**. Irregularly nucleolated small and large lymphoid cells (centrocytes) and scattered histiocytes. (H & E ×100).

126   Follicular depletion in lymph node. (H & E ×10) Follicular depletion is considered a poor prognostic sign and is often seen in the nodes of patients with AIDS. When seen in patients with PGL rapid progression to AIDS frequently occurs.

Section 14: Weight loss

Progressive weight loss may be extremely marked in some patients. This may be related to malabsorption.

127

128

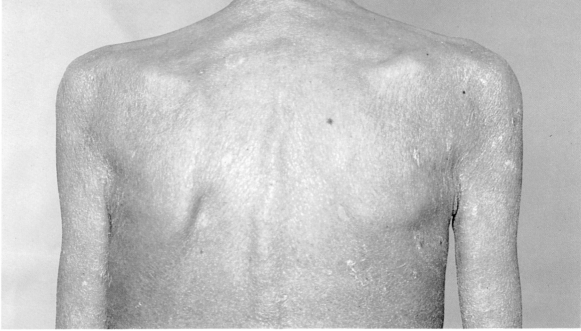

127 and **128**   **Severe wasting** in patient with AIDS.

Section 15: Oral cavity disease

Oral thrush is practically universal in AIDS, and in other patients signals an increased likelihood of developing AIDS. It can usually be treated by topical antifungal preparations but ketoconazole may be required.

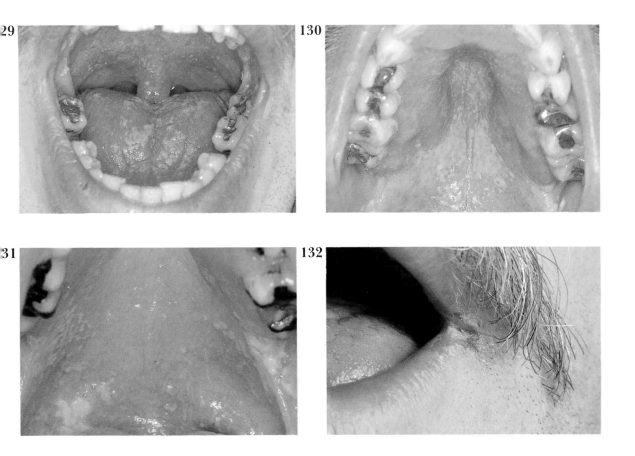

129 to 131 Oral thrush in patients with ARC. Usually white plaques are seen, occasionally the appearance is just of a beefy red oral mucosa.

132 Angular stomatitis, commonly seen in patients with ARC, it is usually associated with oral thrush and responds well to treatment of the thrush and antifungal/hydrocortisone combination creams locally.

Hairy leukoplakia in patients with HTLV III/LAV disease

Hairy leukoplakia was first described in patients with HTLV III/LAV disease. It appears to be due to a proliferation of Epstein-Barr virus, possibly associated with Papilloma virus in the superficial layers of the squamous epithelium of the tongue. In ARC it is usually associated with a poor prognosis. It is seldom symptomatic, but can be treated with keratolytics.

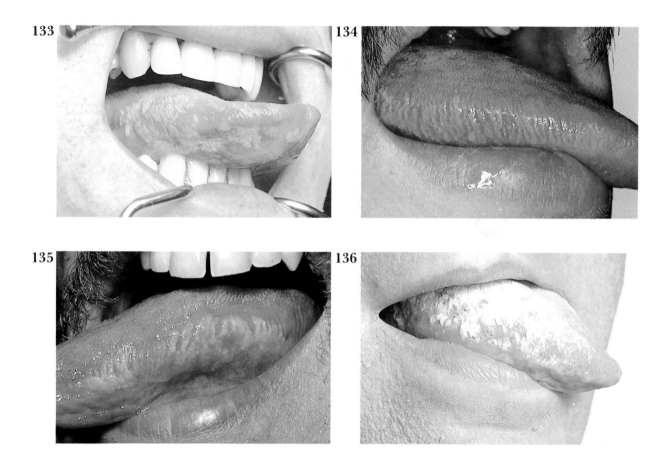

133 to **136** **Hairy leukoplakia** in patients with ARC. Note the distinctive ribbed appearance.

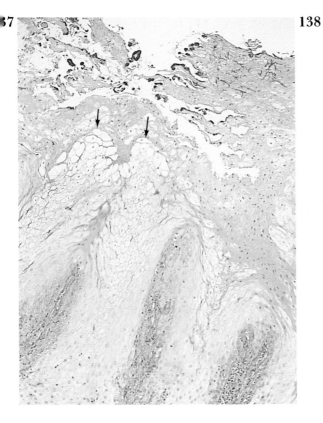

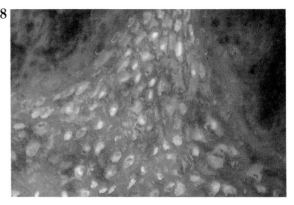

137 Hairy leukoplakia of tongue, showing vacuolated cells (arrows) suggesting viral infection. (H & E ×25)

138 Immunofluorescent preparation using polyclonal antibody against Epstein-Barr virus (EBV) showing positive immunofluorescence in vacuolated cells in upper epithelium (same patient as **142**).

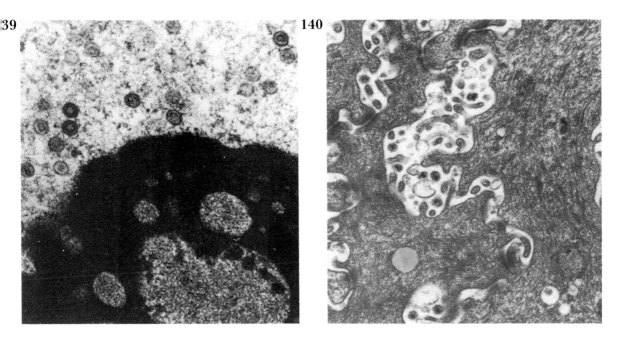

139 Electron micrograph of nucleus of infected squamous epithelial cell, showing condensed chromatin surrounded by multiple EBV particles. (×67,000) (same patient as **133** and **137**).

140 Electron micrograph of intercellular spaces showing multiple EBV particles, some budding from the cell walls. (×28,000) (same patient as **139**).

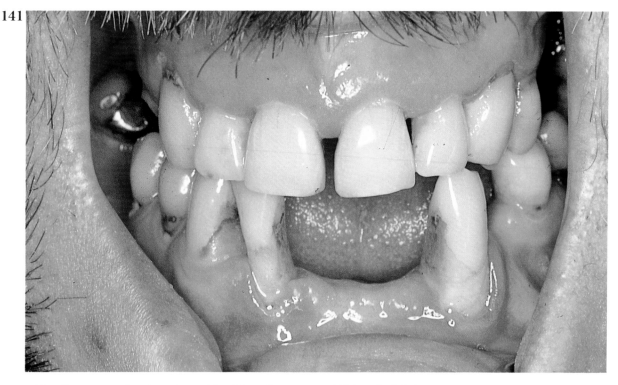

141 Gum recession in patient with ARC, suffering recurrent gingivitis. Gingivitis is almost universal in AIDS and ARC. It responds to treatment with penicillin or metronidazole.

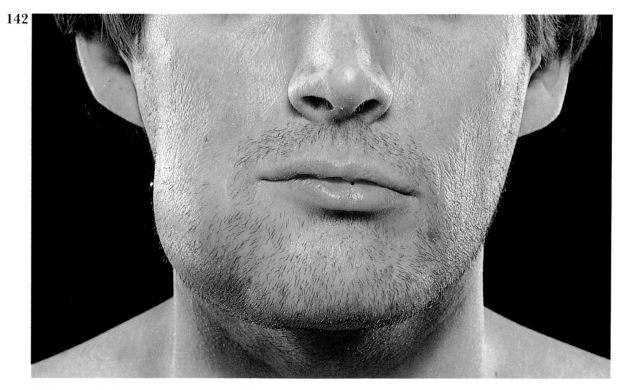

142 Dental abscess in patient with ARC – a common problem.

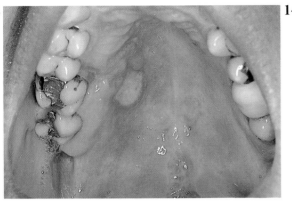

144

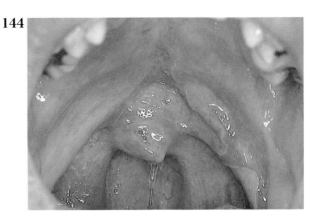

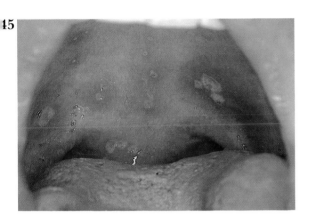

143 to 145 Aphthous ulceration in patients with AIDS. Very severe apthous ulceration occurs in a minority of patients with AIDS and ARC.

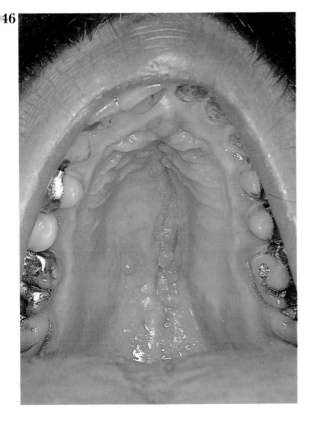

146 Intraoral warts in patient with ARC – an unusual finding.

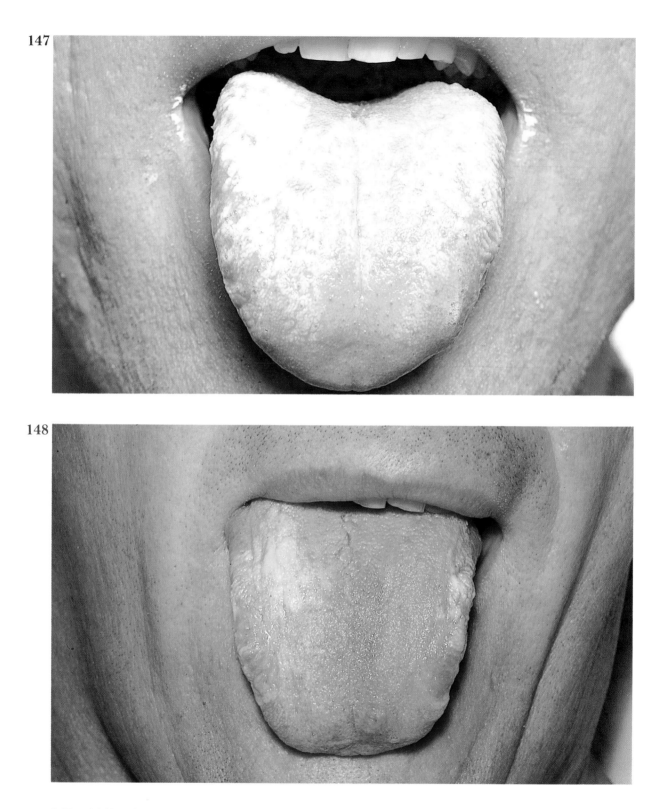

147 and **148** **Coated tongue** in patients with ARC –
a common nonspecific finding.

Section 16: Skin disease

149

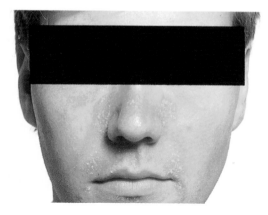

150

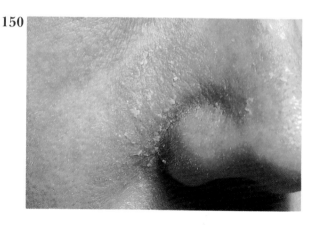

151

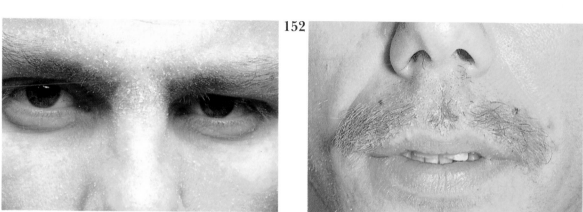

152

149 to 152   Seborrhoeic dermatitis of face. Note typical erythema and scaling in classically affected sites of nasolabial folds, eyebrows and hair-bearing area of upper lip. Seborrhoeic dermatitis is common in the general population, and although not a specific sign of HTLV III/LAV infection, it is often a valuable clinical clue. Severe and extensive seborrhoeic dermatitis in a seropositive patient carries a poor prognosis. The reason for the seborrhoeic dermatitis is as yet unclear but may reflect changes in the cutaneous flora, or the host's reaction to them. The rash responds well to antifungal hydrocortisone creams to the face and stronger corticosteroid creams to the body.

153 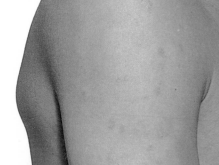 **154**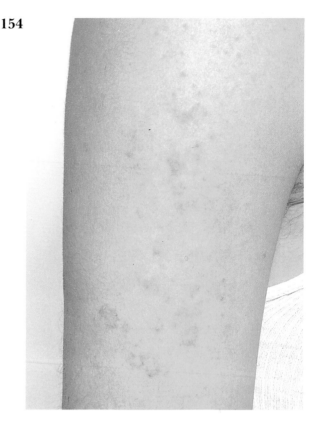

153 and **154** **Nummular seborrhoide on upper arms.** A pattern of seborrhoeic dermatitis seen frequently in patients with HTLV III/LAV disease.

155 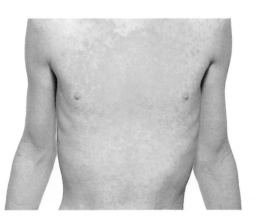 **156**

155 **Seborrhoeic dermatitis of chest,** spreading beyond the usual central sternal area.

156 Close-up of patient in **155**, showing follicular accentuation.

157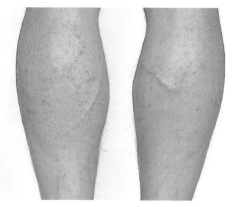

158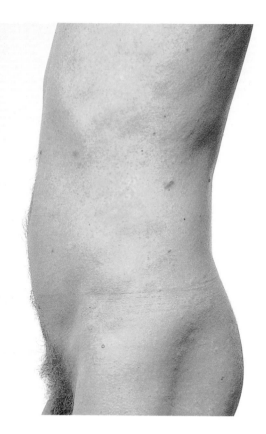

157 and **158** **Extension of follicular dermatitis** beyond the usual seborrhoeic sites.

159 Close-up of **157**.

160 Close-up of patient in **158**.

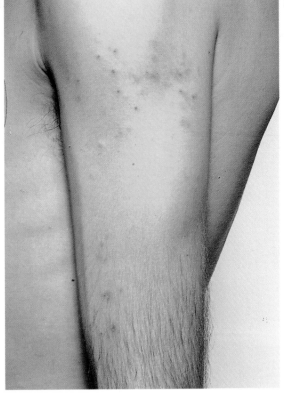 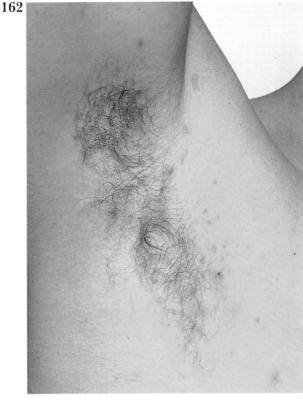

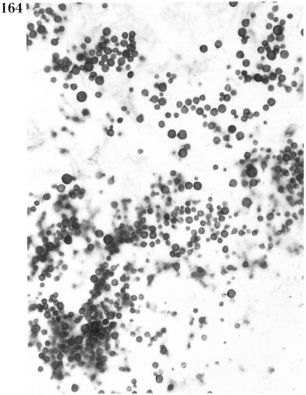

161 to **163** **Typical itchy folliculitis** seen in HTLV III/LAV disease. The lesions are clinically unimpressive, but are often intensely pruritic. They are small and without marked surrounding erythema. The commonest sites are chest, upper arms, lateral neck and face, scalp, axillae and thighs. The folliculitis is usually culture negative but skin scrapings often reveal large numbers of the yeast Pitrosporum orbiculare. Unfortunately, the condition is resistent to treatment, and may cause patients considerable distress. Strong topical corticosteroids and antifungals may provide some relief, but itching may be so severe that antihistamines are required.

164   Blue ink-stained preparation of scraping from the folliculitis, revealing 'Pityrosporum orbiculare'.

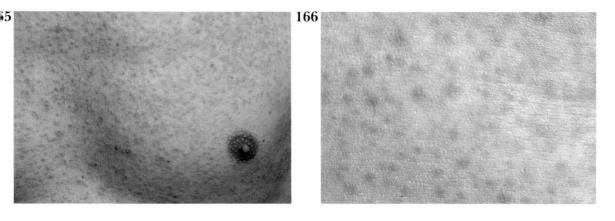

165 and **166**   Extensive folliculitis on chest.

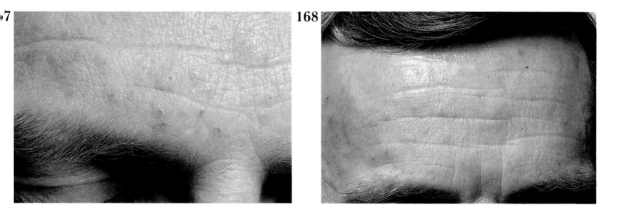

167 and **168**   Excoriated folliculitis of forehead
in two patients, one with AIDS, the other with ARC.

169

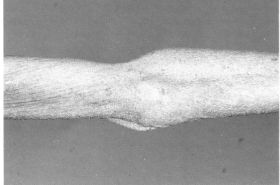

170

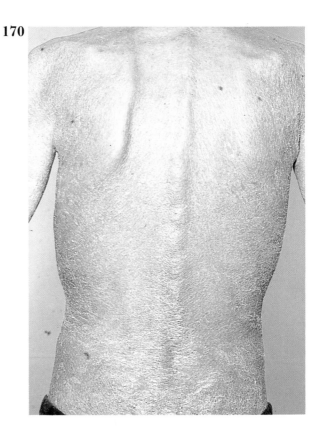

171

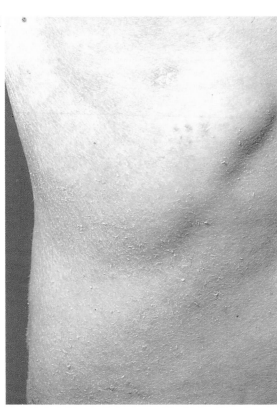

172

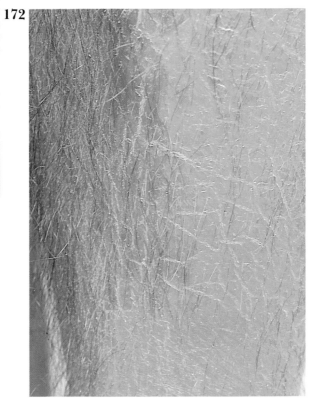

169 to **172** **Xeroderma** in patients with AIDS. Dry skin, particularly over the shins and flanks, is a very common finding in patients with all forms of HTLV III/LAV disease. Patients derive much relief from bath oils, emollient soaps and dry skin creams.

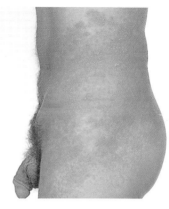

173 and **174** **Herpes zoster.** Shingles is very common, occurring in some 25% of patients with AIDS and ARC. Clinically its course does not appear to be more severe and dissemination is rare. High dose oral acyclovir is helpful if given early.

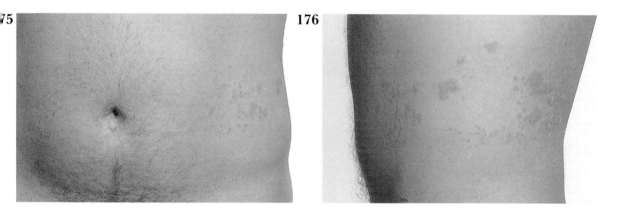

175 and **176** **Herpes zoster** in same patient as **173** and **174** at a later date. A recurrence is not uncommon.

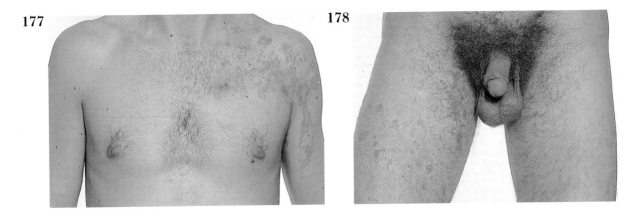

177 and **178**   Herpes zoster occurring simultaneous-
ly in two remote dermatomes in a patient with ARC.

179   Close-up of herpes zoster in right T1
dermatome.

180   Close-up of herpes zoster in right L1/2
dermatomes.

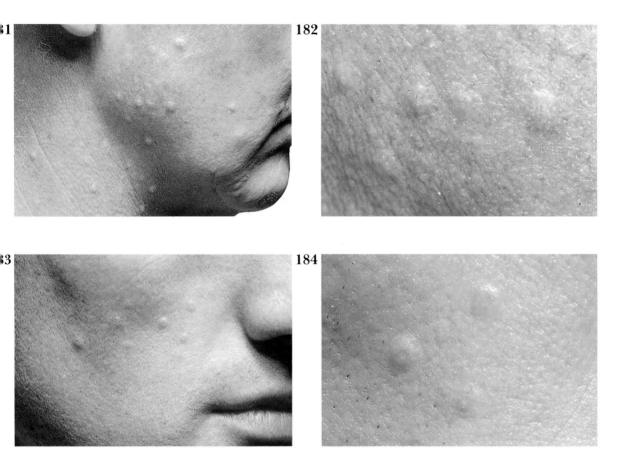

181 to **184 Molluscum contagiosum.** In the
general population this banal superficial pox virus
infection is usually seen in children, especially those
with atopic dermatitis. It may also be seen on the
genitalia in promiscuous young adults. In patients with
HTLV III/LAV disease extensive infections in the
beard area are common, and often recur after local
treatment with phenol.

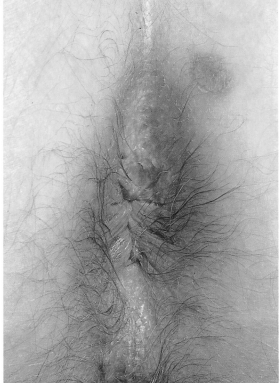

185 **Perianal herpes simplex.** Patients with HTLV III/LAV disease have more severe, persistent or frequently recurrent herpes simplex lesions than normal. Response to oral acyclovir is excellent and it should not be withheld. Maintenance treatment may be required.

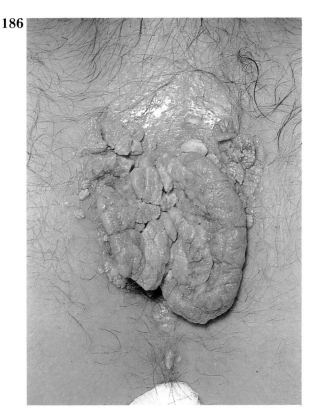

186 **Condyloma acuminata.** Surprisingly, mucocutaneous warts are not often a serious problem in patients with HTLV III/LAV disease. This patient was one particularly bad example.

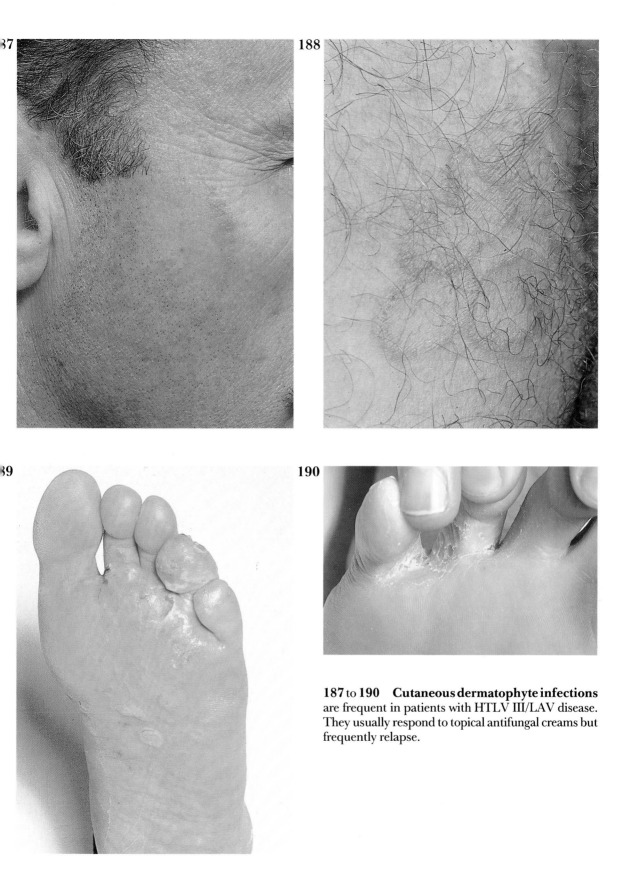

187 to 190 Cutaneous dermatophyte infections are frequent in patients with HTLV III/LAV disease. They usually respond to topical antifungal creams but frequently relapse.

191

192

191 Fungal infection of nails in patient with ARC. A frequent finding.

192 Leukonychia in patient with AIDS. Leukonychia is seen in many severe debilitating diseases.

193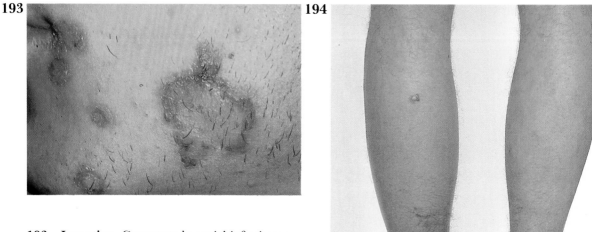

194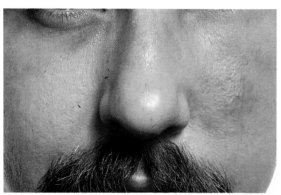

193 Impetigo. Cutaneous bacterial infections are infrequent in patients with HTLV III/LAV disease in comparison to the considerable increase in viral and fungal skin diseases. Impetigo and cellulitis are somewhat more common than in the general adult population.

194 Cellulitis in patient with AIDS, which responded to penicillin but relapsed repeatedly. Note the Kaposi's sarcoma mid calf.

195

195 Cellulitis of the left cheek in patient with ARC, which required intravenous antibiotics before it resolved.

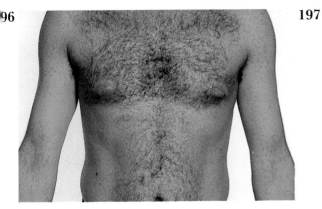

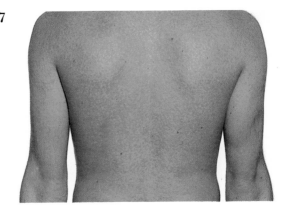

196 and **197** Rash due to cotrimoxazole in patient with PCP. Hypersensitivity to this drug is much more common in patients with HTLV III/LAV disease than in the general population. (See also **31** and **32**.)

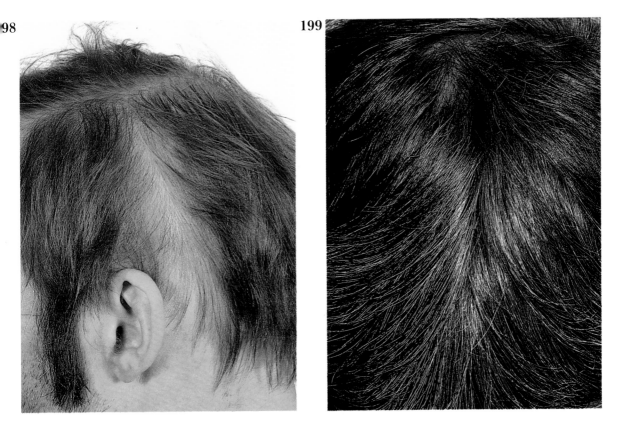

198 **Diffuse alopecia** in patient with AIDS. Hair-fall is a frequent complaint.

199 **Premature greying of hair** is a striking feature in young men with AIDS.

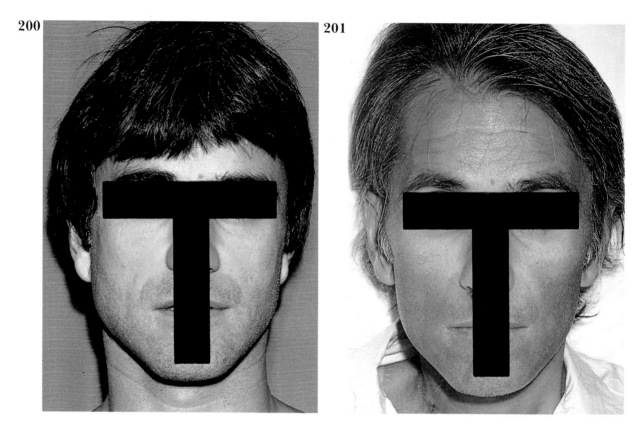

200 and **201**   **Rapid ageing.** These photographs were taken with an interval of two years. Premature greying, frontal recession and thinning of hair, loss of facial fat with hollowing of contour contribute to this appearance.

Other skin diseases which may be associated with HTLV III/LAV disease

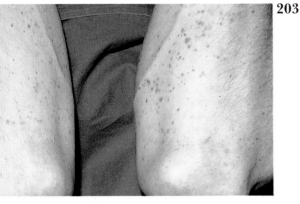

202 and **203** **Cutaneous vasculitis** in patient with AIDS. Several patients have been described with an immune complex vasculitis in AIDS. This is not a frequent finding and seldom leads to systemic vasculitis.

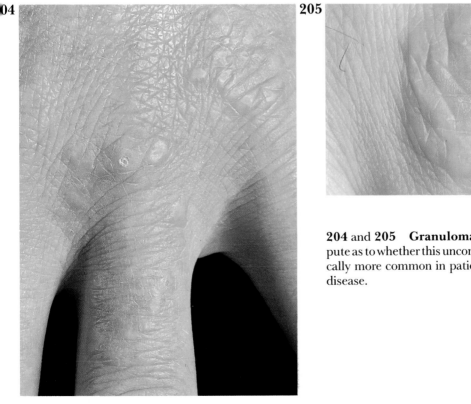

204 and **205** **Granuloma annulare.** There is dispute as to whether this uncommon condition is statistically more common in patients with HTLV III/LAV disease.

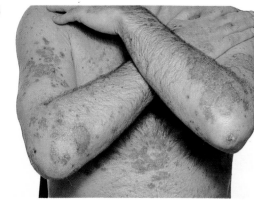

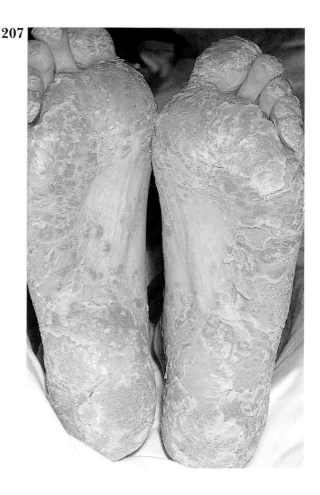

206 and **207**   **Psoriasis may** be more severe after HTLV III/LAV infection. Both these patients were seropositive.

Section 17: ENT problems

Sinusitis and allergic rhinitis, are very frequent problems in patients with HTLV III/LAV disease. The sinusitis responds to conventional antibiotic therapy but the allergic rhinitis may be difficult to control. It frequently causes post nasal drip and 'catarrh' and patients may complain of vomiting secondary to their catarrh. Corticosteroid/topical antibiotic nasal sprays may provide relief. Interestingly the nasal mucosa in these patients has a granulomatous appearance.

Part 4   Other sexually transmitted diseases in HTLV III/LAV positive patients

When following HTLV III/LAV positive patients it is important to monitor for other sexually transmitted diseases.

Interestingly in this group syphilis may be missed as the VDRL can be negative or in low titre (see **208**). Otherwise the manifestations of syphilis are no different from usual.

It seems that this group of patients is particularly vulnerable to the herpes viruses (see **34, 110** and **173**). Hepatitis B infection seems not to be unusually severe, however. Hepatitis B vaccination should probably be given to all HTLV III/LAV positive patients at risk. Antibody response to the vaccine may be impaired.

208

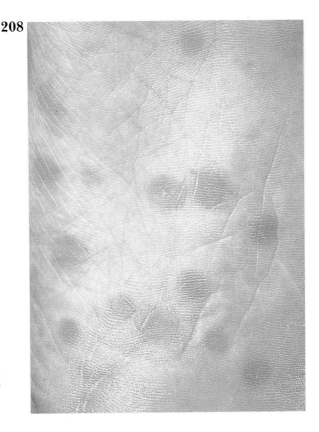

208   Secondary syphilis in patient with AIDS. This patient with florid secondary syphilis had a VDRL titre of only 1:2.

Part 5   Counselling of patients with HTLV III/LAV disease

No book on AIDS would be complete without discussion of the psychological as well as the strictly medical needs of the patients.

Few diseases are as frightening to patients as AIDS and yet, as well as the fear of death, they often have to face a cruel rejection by their friends and society. Many homosexual patients may develop AIDS or ARC before they have come to terms with their own homosexuality and they must also face up to this and work through feelings of guilt that may cause them to suffer even more.

It is important, if patients are going to be able to cope, that their doctors talk openly and honestly to them about their condition and, if appropriate, about their guilt and the fact that they might be dying. The greatest complaint from patients is that they are not told enough about their disease. The situation can even arise where patients know more about their disease than their doctors. They want to know so much about what they can do to help themselves, how they can prevent transmitting the disease to others and what treatments are available to them – and they should be given time to discuss these matters. A detailed handout is a useful adjunct – it enables the patient to review the facts outside the doctor's office where stress means that much of what is said is forgotten.

Counselling is particularly important when it comes to the use of the HTLV III/LAV antibody test. It is vital that if this test is to be performed on relatively well patients that they understand that it is a test which indicates the likely presence of the AIDS virus, and that a positive result does not in itself mean AIDS. Except in unusual circumstances this test should not be performed without the knowledge and consent of the patient and the result should be treated in the strictest confidence. A patient receiving a positive result may require considerable counselling and certainly deserves detailed information. The physician may often have to prescribe for symptoms of the hyperventilation syndrome and irritable bowel syndrome, so marked is the anxiety. The best treatment for these however, is probably a sympathetic ear and a promise of support.

Part 6 Transmission and prevention of HTLV III/LAV disease

The principal means of transmission of HTLV III/LAV infection are anal and/or vaginal intercourse and the sharing of intravenous needles and 'gear' by drug addicts. Blood and blood product transfusion did account for some 2% of cases early in the epidemic. However, the screening of blood donations with the HTLV III/LAV antibody test, and the heat treatment of factor VIII, have essentially eliminated these modes of transmission. Other forms of sexual activity such as oral sex, although possible routes of transmission, appear to carry considerably less risk.

It would appear that trauma in sexual intercourse is not required for the transmission of the virus, as artificial insemination of semen alone has been responsible for infection in humans and other primates.

The risk of transmission of HTLV III/LAV to health workers appears to be extremely low. The only significant risk seems to be needle stick injury with actual injection of contaminated fluid. Seroconversion has been documented after a needle stick injury, which involved injection of infected blood. Several hundred subjects have been followed after simple needle prick injuries without seroconversion or the development of AIDS. A Vacutainer system excludes the possibility of injection of fluids following needle prick injury. Needles should be immediately discarded into a sharps bin without resheathing, or removal from the Vacutainer holder/syringe, unless some form of extra protection device such as 'Needle Guard' is attached to the sheath (210).*

Other precautions that should be taken are always to ensure that the patient is lying down for venepuncture to avoid syncope, and to have the sharps bin close to hand. Gloves should be worn whenever dealing with body fluids, and spills should be mopped up using sodium hypochlorite (212) as a disinfectant. During all operative procedures the only additional precaution to the usual gloves, gowns and masks that perhaps should be used is eye protection, although aerosol or splash injury to the conjunctiva has not been documented as a mode of transmission. Instruments are adequately sterilised by heat. Instruments that cannot be subjected to heat are best sterilised using glutaraldehyde which renders HTLV III/LAV harmless very quickly. A half hour submersion is probably adequate.

*Needle Guard is supplied by Bio Safe Products Ltd., PO Box 5350, Auckland, New Zealand.

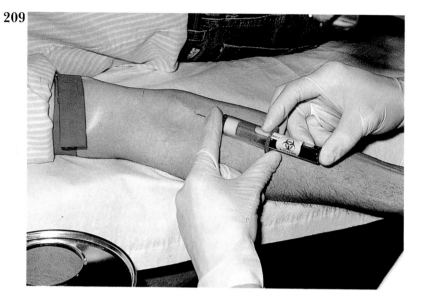

209 **Venepuncture** in patient with AIDS.

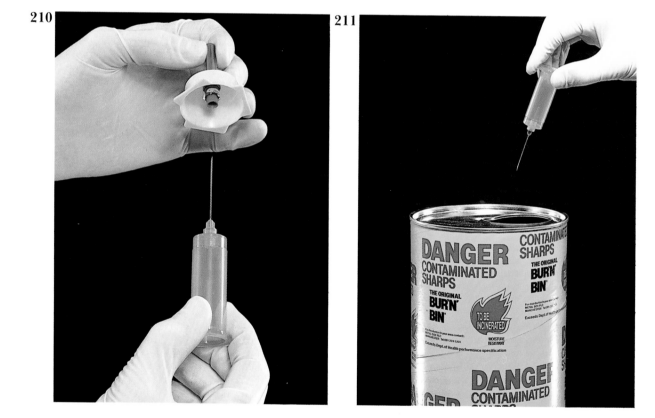

210 **Disposal of needle with safety guard.**

211 **Sharps bin.**

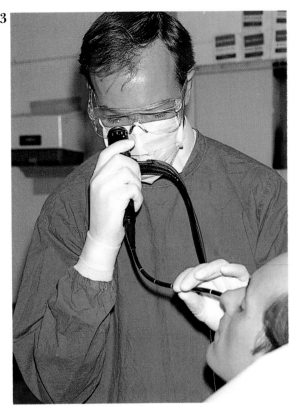

212 Hypochlorite for mopping up spilled blood.

213 Fibreoptic bronchoscopy being performed with operator wearing eye protection.

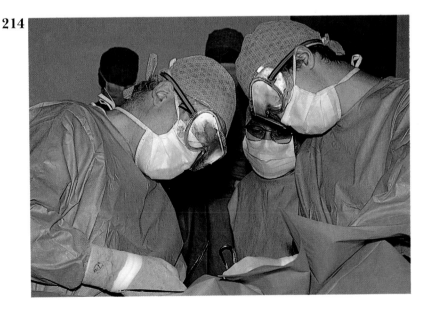

214 Lymph node biopsy being performed. Surgeons wearing eye protection.

Abbreviations

AIDS –   Acquired immunodeficiency syndrome

ARC –   AIDS-related complex

CMV –   Cytomegalovirus

CDC –   Center for Disease Control

EBV –   Epstein-Barr virus

ELISA –   Enzyme-linked immunosorbent assay

H & E –   Haematoxylin and eosin

HTLV –   Human T-cell lymphotropic virus

LAV –   Lymphadenopathy-associated virus

PCP –   Pneumocystis carinii pneumonia

PGL –   Persistent generalised lymphadenopathy

RIPA –   Radio-immune precipitin assay

XLD –   Xylose Lysine Desoxycholate agar

Index